Islamic Values and Management Practices

Transformation and Innovation Series

Series Editors:
Ronnie Lessem, University of Buckingham, UK
Alexander Schieffer, University of St. Gallen, Switzerland

This series on enterprise transformation and social innovation comprises a range of books informing practitioners, consultants, organization developers, development agents and academics how businesses and other organizations, as well as the discipline of economics itself, can and will have to be transformed. The series prepares the ground for viable twenty-first entury enterprises and a sustainable macroeconomic system. A new kind of R&D, involving social, as well as technological innovation, needs to be supported by integrated and participative action research in the social sciences. Focusing on new, emerging kinds of public, social and sustainable entrepreneurship originating from all corners of the world and from different cultures, books in this series will help those operating at the interface between enterprise and society to mediate between the two and will help schools teaching management and economics to re-engage with their founding principles.

Current titles in this series

Transformation Management
Towards the Integral Enterprise
Ronnie Lessem and Alexander Schieffer
ISBN 978-0-566-08896-4

Integral Research and Innovation
Transforming Enterprise and Society
Ronnie Lessem and Alexander Schieffer
ISBN 978-0-566-08918-3

Integral Economics
Releasing the Economic Genius of Your Society
Ronnie Lessem and Alexander Schieffer
ISBN 978-0-566-09247-3

Finance at the Threshold
Rethinking the Real and Financial Economies
Christopher Houghton Budd
ISBN 978-0-566-09211-4

Culture and Economics in the Global Community:
A Framework for Socioeconomic Development
Kensei Hiwaki
ISBN 978-1-4094-0412-5

Islamic Values and Management Practices

Quality and Transformation in the Arab World

MAQBOULEH M. HAMMOUDEH

Routledge
Taylor & Francis Group

LONDON AND NEW YORK

First published 2012 by Gower Publishing

Published 2016 by Routledge
2 Park Square, Milton Park, Abingdon, Oxfordshire OX14 4RN
711 Third Avenue, New York, NY 10017, USA

First issued in paperback 2016

Routledge is an imprint of the Taylor & Francis Group, an informa business

Gower Applied Business Research
Our programme provides leaders, practitioners, scholars and researchers with thought provoking, cutting edge books that combine conceptual insights, interdisciplinary rigour and practical relevance in key areas of business and management.

British Library Cataloguing in Publication Data
Hammoudeh, Maqbouleh M.
 Islamic values and management practices : quality and
 transformation in the Arab world. -- (Transformation and
 innovation)
 1. Management--Religious aspects--Islam.
 2. Organizational change. 3. Organizational change--
 Islamic countries. 4. Total quality management. 5. Total
 quality management--Islamic countries. 6. Business
 ethics--Islamic countries.
 I. Title II. Series
 658'.0088297-dc22

Library of Congress Cataloging-in-Publication Data
Hammoudeh, Maqbouleh M.
 Islamic values and management practices : quality and transformation in
 the Arab world / by Maqbouleh M. Hammoudeh.
  p. cm.
 Includes bibliographical references and index.
 ISBN 978-1-4094-0752-2 (hardback) -- ISBN 978-1-4094-0753-9
 (ebook) 1. Management--Arab countries. 2. Management--Religious
 aspects--Islam. 3. Work--Religious aspects--Islam. 4. Values (Islam) I. Title.
 HD70.A64H36 2011
 658.0088'297--dc23

                                                              2011027138

ISBN 13: 978-1-138-26986-6 (pbk)
ISBN 13: 978-1-4094-0752-2 (hbk)

Contents

List of Figures and Tables

Preface

Maqbouleh Hammoudeh is the first management consultant, educator, researcher and practitioner in the Arab world in contemporary times to co-evolve and subsequently apply an approach to management that draws on and develops, explicitly, Islamic philosophies and practices.

Originating from Prophet Mohammad, and subsequently evolved for contemporary purposes by her consulting colleague Dr Assaf, so-called I.Theory – I. for simultaneously Islamic and international – has been taken forward and applied by Hammoudeh in the public, private and civic sectors, currently in Jordan, and prospectively in the Arab world. It is a way of bringing balance and justice to the forefront of management in the Arab world and of focusing on Islamic values.

We are personally extremely proud of what Maqbouleh has accomplished in this book. She has done an amazing piece of work in bringing an Islamic approach to management into both the local and global arenas.

We believe that this book represents a giant step forward for all management practitioners in the Arab world in achieving organisational objectives in quality and transformation, as illustrated by the two case studies featured in it. The first one concerns the development of the Royal Society for Conservation of Nature in Jordan and the second is about the growth within and of the Al-Quds Paints Co. as a producer in Jordan's industrial sector. Each of these organisations sees itself as a 'values-managed organisation'.

For this social innovation, Maqbouleh Hammoudeh has been awarded a doctorate by Geneva-based TRANS4M, an internationally active institute of higher learning and a senior evaluation council for social innovation, comprised of internationally respected academics from around the world and outstanding representatives from Jordanian society.

Professor Ronnie Lessem
Dr Alexander Schieffer
Series Editors

Acknowledgment

I would like to thank all those who supported me and provided me with all the necessary information, especially my Co-operative Inquiry Team in RSCN and Al-Quds Paints Co., and my editor, Majd Muhsen, whose efforts were instrumental in producing this book.

To my mother, who prayed day and night for me to be my best.

To my son and daughters, who encouraged me to achieve my hopes, against all the odds.

To Dr Assaf, the author of I.Theory.

To my professor, Dr Ronnie Lessem, who urged me to write this book.

Reviews for
Islamic Values and
Management Practices

...successfully combines the classical Islamic theoretical perspectives towards Management generally and Human Resource Management particularly with the related contemporary theoretical and methodological perspectives that led to produce a blueprint for guiding Management Development and Human Resource Management transformational programs which are compatible with Arab World and Middle East socio-cultural contexts.

The author's acknowledged long standing expertise as Management consultant and trainer in Jordan and in the Arab World and the successful implementation of the developed blueprint in various organizations in Jordan add to the credibility of this book.

Adel Al-Rasheed, Professor of Management, German Jordanian University
and Yarmouk University in Jordan

Dr. Hammoudeh's work is a testimony for the imperative for knowledge mining in Islamic culture to inform and enlighten the Business literature and practice. Her insights on the linkages between culture and business are of value since her model has resonance with basic notions of Tawheed *(Unity),* Ihsan *(inner beauty) and* Mizan *(social justice). There are windows of opportunities to harness and embody local knowledge inspired by Islamic values as a humanitarian and universal business charter that will both enhance cultural diversity and innovation through sound and smart understanding of text and context in both Islam and Business.*

Prof. Odeh Al-Jayyousi, Regional Director, IUCN

This book, takes you through several journeys to explore and help you live the experience of management in Islam through the personal journey of the author, the transformation journey of two local organizations, the journey of total quality management in Jordan to the journey of consulting in an Arabic country. For sure, one thing Maqbouleh is not going to deprive from: the inquisitiveness to learn and find more about the fascinating subjects she succeeded to open widely for research and reflection.

Zain E A M Tahboub, Ph.D., Researcher, Consultant and Strategy Adviser

Reading Dr. Maqboulah Hammoudeh's book, I admired her courageous approach to I.Theory. She provoked my intelligence to read more about management in Islam as tactics and strategy, and about objectives and means by which to attain quality transformation. As a secular educationist, it was an unprecedented approach to take the lead and dig deeply into this sensitive subject which is a taboo dominated by religious thought in this part of the World. While reading through the book, I admired her simplicity in delivering the I.Theory's core and concept, considering balance and justice as means of development and transformation.

Dr Hammoudeh's work will attract more researches in this untapped field.

Mohammad Shahin, CEO, JOSWE Medical, Amman, Jordan

This book is extremely important and unique as it examines Islam from a management and social dimension which has been neglected, even though it was the main contribution to human development for decades. I hope this book will provoke further use of the principles of Islam in the revitalization of human cvilisation.

Yehya Khaled, Director General, The Royal Society for the
Conservation of Nature (RSCN), Jordan

Context

Context

1 *Orientation*

This introductory chapter presents a detailed summary of the 12 chapters of the book.

Part 1: Context

BURNING QUESTIONS

At a time when the world in general, and the Arab world in particular, is awakening, if not still in despair, this book introduces 'management by values', using 'I. (Islamic and International) Theory', specifically in relation to quality and transformation. I shall be focusing on this as a means to improving the quality of life and work in the Arab world of the basis of Islamic values. The aim of this approach, which I am exploring in both my personal life and in my professional work, is to search for new means of unification between individuals and organisations in Jordan and the Middle East. Through this new perspective I hope to serve both business and society, and to make of use my own personal and business journey in order to implement total quality in Jordanian and Arab organisations and a better quality of life in a turbulent environment. My aim is to review 'I.Theory' and its implementation in management based on culture, including values and, most importantly, the alignment between employees and senior management.

In this regard, I shall address two burning questions:

1. How can we develop a management theory based on Islamic values that will lead to greater quality and transformation in Arab organisations?
2. What is the specific role of I.Theory in supporting the development of a local identity towards global integrity?

My chief objective is thus to apply a management theory to Jordanian and Arab organisations that is based on Islamic values and culture rather than on Western management theories, with a view to achieving an authentic transformation, starting on a local level, but with a view to the global.

I.Theory stands for an Islamic management model. Using case studies of the Royal Society for the Conservation of Nature (RSCN) (a civil society organisation) and Al-Quds Paints Co. (a business), it will be demonstrated how individual culture and organisational culture can be aligned and the security of societal culture can be achieved.

Enterprises in the Middle East currently face urgent concerns and challenges in matters of organisational sustainability, quality of life and total quality management (TQM). Therefore, they may need to reconsider their ways of thinking in order to become more attuned with our genuine values and culture, particularly at this time of so-called 'Arab Awakening'.

THE STORY SO FAR

In Chapter 2, I will set this book in the context of the emerging – or indeed awakening – self, organisation and society, beginning with my own story.

My own story

I was born into a Palestinian family in a small Palestinian town in 1947. This was a catastrophic year for the Palestinian people, which led to our becoming refugees in neighbouring Arab countries, in Jordan in particular, where my family ended up during that earliest period of my life.

I graduated in 1969 with a bachelor's degree in Economics and Statistics, and hoped that one day I would become a minister of planning and implement development strategies for the lagging Jordanian economy. I was also encouraged by my father's immortal saying: 'A penny saved is a penny earned'. He would quote from the holy Qur'an, and always urged us to avoid waste in every possible way. During my university studies, the second Arab–Israeli war erupted, in June 1967, and more Palestinian refugees flooded into Jordan. This had severe repercussions for both the economy and our people, and I wondered how we could build societies and achieve any progress while wars were erupting every 10 or 20 years. Against the odds, I struggled to create a position for myself and embarked on my career.

From 1970 until now, I have worked in education and in management consultancy in the whole of the Arab region, most specifically in Jordan. I worked first as a teacher of girls in Yemen and Libya, and in mixed schools in Algeria. I faced many challenges in all of these countries, especially in Algeria, where I found the language to be a problem.

After eight years as an expatriate, I decided that it was time to return home and start drawing more purposefully on my beliefs and principles in order to build upon the economic and management disciplines that I had previously taught in community colleges in Amman. These principles of mine are strongly based on mastery (*Itqan*) in Islam, which not only emphasises the quality of performance but also displays its ethical and spiritual context, as stated by Prophet Mohammad: '*Allah loves to see one's job done at the level of Itqan*' (Saheeh Muslim).

The organisation in which I work

In 1984 I joined TEAM (Transport, Engineering and Management) International consultants, a Cairo-based pan-Arab management and engineering consultancy. I discovered, at least initially, that TEAM and I shared the same objectives and philosophy. It was a great opportunity for me to implement my own beliefs and thinking with regard to sustainable organisations and organisational development in general, to elevate the level of professional services and to introduce socio-political navigation into our Arab organisations. However, what I had not thought through at that time was that such navigation was more Western than Islamic or Arab in orientation.

In 1995, TEAM (Jordan) began to offer its customers the ISO 9000 quality management system as the first step towards implementing TQM in their organisations. We were relating a global quality approach (ISO 9000) to a local culture, rather than evolving a local approach with a view to making it more global. This was to come later, through I.Theory, which I was to co-evolve in my doctoral work.

Nevertheless, we were pioneers in Jordan and managed to export this service to the majority of TEAM branches around the Arab world. The ISO 9001 and ISO 9002 quality management systems were very necessary for organisations, helping them to document their procedures and providing them with clear guidelines to follow.

In a further development, we signed an agreement with the University of Buckingham to run its master's programme in Transformation Management. This was ostensibly to promote organisational learning and knowledge creation in organisations in the Middle East. Participants and organisations, myself and TEAM (Jordan) included, underwent a process of transformation in which they grounded themselves in Arab and Islamic culture, with a view to transforming themselves from a local–global perspective.

As we shall see, the co-operative inquiry teams at RSCN (where the management director was a graduate of the Transformation Management programme) and Al Quds Paints Co. are living examples of the transformation that we are promoting. Today TEAM (Jordan), my consultancy company, is eager to promote and see the results of I.Theory, that is, management by (Islamic) values. We believe that ours is the only consultancy company in the Arab world today that is doing this.

My society

Jordan is a small county. The population is of mixed origins, due to past and present wars (including Arab–Israeli wars and US–Iraqi wars). This turbulent environment has led to instability and insecurity throughout the Middle East region, and Jordan has been significantly affected by it. Because it is a country of limited natural resources, it has been essential, over the past decades, for Jordan to transform itself from a so-called 'underdeveloped' desert kingdom. It therefore became a priority for entrepreneurs and people in general to start building more fully functional, values-oriented organisations, with a special emphasis on their long-term sustainability.

Yet, people observe double standards on a daily basis. They believe in management by values, but at the same time they feel that these values do not matter so much when they see successful organisations behaving unethically – or worse, when powerful and influential people create havoc in the world while preaching the good news.

During the past decade the government of Jordan has joined up with the World Bank to come up with reform strategies so as to create improvements in different sectors. However, the focus of these strategies is chiefly technological and economic, and there is scant regard for cultural, ethical and spiritual matters. Modernisation, as currently portrayed in Jordan, is somehow modest and shallow – to a great extent lacking in important features such as delegation, proper systems and even professional relations between managers (Al-Rasheed, 2001).

FROM MANAGEMENT CONSULTING TO AL SHURA

In Chapter 3, I pose the following critical questions: How can we, as management consultants, help organisations to achieve organisational transformation and a better quality of life? How can we facilitate the transformation process inside the organisation? What values should top management espouse in order to achieve quality and transformation? Here, the value on which I draw in particular is *Al Shura* (consultation) in Islam. One definition of *Al Shura* is negotiation and dialogue to reveal what is right. The aim is to know what is correct, after first becoming acquainted with all the elements of a particular issue and considering numerous points of view.

Al Shura is to submit difficult problems in worldly and religious affairs to people who are known for their wide practical experience and wise advice. It is to listen to different opinions and deduce suitable solutions (Al-Tamimi, 2003).

As a management consultant, I believe that our role not only entails corporate diagnosis, but can actually extend to include social aspects as well. Therefore, we can address certain social problems that may have significant effects on the corporate life cycle, since we are both targeting organisational sustainability and, most importantly, aiming to achieve a better quality of life.

Part 2: Methodology

METHODOLOGY

In Chapter 4, I explain why I use the co-operative inquiry methodology developed by John Heron and how it helps in achieving the main objectives described in this book – self-, organisational and societal renewal, within a framework of epistemology and knowledge.

Method

I also draw on case-study methods to review the application of I.Theory in the RSCN, a non-profit organisation, and Al-Quds Paints Co., a small factory aiming to achieve the required transformation. This method is compatible with the co-operative inquiry methodology: it covers the contextual conditions and answers the main questions in this book.

CO-OPERATIVE INQUIRY METHODOLOGY

Co-operative inquiry as a methodology was developed by John Heron (Heron, 1996). His approach is based on the democratic participation of the individual within a group. It involves two or more people researching and developing a topic or area of concern and using a series of cycles in which they move between action and reflection. The methodology is distinctive in its co-operative approach. It includes four ways of knowing: Experiential, Imaginal or Presentational, Propositional and Practical. These were applied in both the RSCN and the Al-Quds Paints Co.

The knowledge modes conceived by Heron are quite distinct, and take us on to a particular and transformative mode of thought, and ultimately to action.

The epistemic perspective

The epistemic side of this paradigm is about participative knowing. This experiential knowing involves the following, as per John Heron's *Co-operative Inquiry*:

- Participation through empathetic communion and imagining, whereby knowing is mutual and awakening.
- Participation in anything explicitly is to participate in everything tacitly.
- The distinction between participative and non-participative knowing, in which the knower splits subject from object.
- Integration of the three stages which reflect the human stages from childhood to ego development, then to mature integration.
- Holism of inquiry, grounded in participative knowing.

The political perspective

This perspective holds that the subjects participate as researchers in the inquiry process, including the generation of knowledge, decision making and so on. This is based on the idea that people have the right to participate in decisions that affect their lives, in accordance with the principles of democratisation and empowerment.

As we shall see in the case studies, RSCN and Al-Quds Paints Co. began to adopt the participatory approach in every decision in order to germinate the democracy indicated in John Heron's *Co-operative Inquiry*, thus building confidence and quality in order to transform their respective organisations and create organisations 'managed by values' derived from local roots and a culture based on Islamic values and ethics.

Part 3: Content

FROM TOTALITY QUALITY MANAGEMENT TO I.THEORY

The backbone of this book is the theory (Part 3), which consists of six chapters related to quality of life from an Islamic perspective. It covers subjects such as TQM as a lifestyle based on *Itqan* (perfection) in Islam and transformation. It also includes a comparison between Islamic theory in management (I.Theory) and Western and Japanese theories, as well as Islamic values and my role in evolving the I.Theory in terms of its implementation on both cultural and systems levels in Jordanian organisations.

TOTAL QUALITY MANAGEMENT IN AMERICA AND JAPAN

In Chapter 5, I focus on TQM and its features. The chapter covers the history of Total Quality (TQ), which commenced in the Muslim world in the days of Prophet Mohammad (Peace be upon him) and is related to his sayings about *Itqan* (perfection). I also include other philosophers, such as the American W.E. Deming, and discuss Deming's principles and how we can improve quality according to his chain reaction and the 14 points that he drew up to help people transform their businesses (Deming, 1986).

Deming believed that in order to achieve TQM, management should base systems on statistical quality controls, on the one hand, and that there should be continuous improvement and progressive product development efforts, on the other hand, in manufacturing processes. He also stressed that top management needs to be firm and consistent in terms of commitment and compliance and that, most importantly, it should assume total responsibility for quality improvement.

J.M. Juran, on the other hand, focused on customer satisfaction and the importance of having deficiency-free products in order to avoid customer dissatisfaction (Rampersad, 2005).

But philosophers have different approaches to the implementation organisational change by targeting development and sustainability.

As for Japanese TQ philosophers, Ishikawa and Taguchi introduced principles such as quality planning, quality control, the Ishikawa diagram (fishbone diagram) and quality improvement.

Ishikawa built and promoted greater involvement of top management than of front-line staff and reduced the reliance on quality professionals and quality departments. And while Taguchi explained the economic value of reducing variation, he maintained and measured quality as a variation from the target value of design specification and translated it in economic terms (loss function) that express the cost of variation in monetary terms.

Despite the implementation of TQM in the West or the East, we need an Islamic theory that reflects our culture and value system. I.Theory has features that have evolved from our history, ideology and religion that could enhance the chances of successful TQM practice. These features include *Tawheed* (unification of individuals with the group), *Itqan* (perfection) and justice, as will be explained later. This could provide a satisfying answer to my first question: How can we develop a management theory that is based on our culture rather than on Western theories and that can be implemented within our organisations?

QUALITY IN ISLAM

In Chapter 6, I discuss the origins of quality practices in Islam, such as *Shura* (consultation), and the meaning of *Itqan* (perfection) as quality of work as well as quality of life. I also cover the work of some Muslim scholars who talk about quality and ethics. For example, the *Hisba* system, which is a quality and control system, and the features of *Almuhtasib* (inspector) are presented as elements of the quality system in Islam. Further, the documentation system in the Islamic state, called *Dawaween*, is similar to information management and control systems. I also make a comparison between Islamic quality and the modern approach in quality (ISO 9000) and TQM.

At the end of Chapter 6, I point out that, despite the many successful cases associated with the implementation of ISO 9000, there is still substantial criticism of it. For example, John Seddon (1997) has built a critique based on the erroneous philosophy of ISO 9000, which, according to him, focuses on commands and control rather than improvement and development. However, I believe that we should study all management theories and, at the same time, develop our own, based on our culture and religion, to promote the quality and transformation we yearn for.

MANAGERIAL PHILOSOPHY: COMPARATIVE APPROACH

In Chapters 7 and 8, I review management philosophy from a comparative perspective. In Chapter 7, I compare and contrast the development of management philosophies prior to the Industrial Revolution. The first management approach was that of 'management by sufficiency' (which means following rules and regulations), which then evolved into management by efficiency, which is sufficiency plus an initiative to innovate and create.

These management philosophies are still applied in the West. However, the third philosophy in which I am interested is management by effectiveness, which is based, for me, on values and culture. It also means efficiency plus two major elements: First is the unification of objectives among individuals (employees) and the group (management) and society. Second is continuous improvement based on initiative, innovation and creation. This is, basically, the essence of the Islamic Theory (I.Theory) that was developed first by my colleague Dr Abdelmutti Assaf, and thereafter by me, whereby we developed the concepts of I.Theory in management, based on management by values and culture.

ISLAMIC THEORY

In Chapter 9, I focus specifically on I.Theory, which is based on a number of principles, including:

1. The need to build human organisations, socially and politically as well as commercially. Such organisations should be comprised of many elements, with the human being at their centre. Related to that should be a value system, forming the moral basis of the organisation.
2. Justice is the ultimate value in I.Theory. It is one thing that every organisation cannot do without, because the Islamic concept of justice is derived from divine guidance. In one of his aphorisms, Ali Ibn Abu Talib (the last of the four caliphs who ruled after Prophet Mohammad's death) said: 'Justice puts everything in its place' (Nasr, 2004). Justice is related to balance, and to giving each thing its due (*Haqq*). It is having everything in its own place according to its nature, and it is a divine requirement to search for balance in our lives.
3. The need to identify the management value systems that comply with the model's core value. Such compliance with values is necessary to guarantee harmony and avoid conflict of interests between business owners and workers.

I.Theory relies on effectiveness, which means efficiency plus two major elements:

*   unifying organisational objectives with those of employees
*   making sure that continuous improvement is seen through a total strategic view, and for the long run.

The context of I.Theory leads to co-operation as an Islamic value. For Muslims, the justice value in the life of any organisation is the ultimate value, which brings balance between the soul and spirit of the individual, on the one hand, and the soul and spirit of the group, on the other. Table 1.1 summarises the differences between I.Theory and Western and Eastern management theories.

Table 1.1   Comparison between I.Theory and Western and Eastern management theories, based on management styles

	I.Theory	West*	East (Japan)
Value	Justice	Individual freedom	Social equality
Interest	Unification of individual and group interest	Individual interest	Group interest
Style of management	Management by effectiveness	Management by sufficiency and efficiency	Management by effectiveness
Management environment	Co-operative environment	Conflict and competition	Co-operative environment

* By 'West', I refer mainly to the USA.

Source: Developed by researcher

From a philosophical point of view, the main element of I.Theory is *Al Tawheed* (oneness), which can be translated as 'unification' or the act of uniting or bringing together all that is conflicted or paradoxical in order to create harmony. The unification process allows for genuine compatibility between each group or organisation and the goals of individuals within such groups. This cannot be achieved without real and total unification of the duality (individual and group).

Achieving unification at all levels, from an Islamic point of view, requires building systems according to specific norms and regulations. In all universal phenomena, there are many rules and regulations that are used to build systems with precision and accuracy. Likewise, there are flexible and dynamic elements for building systems and regulations in a society in order to achieve quality and sustainability. These regulations are based on Islam and aim to protect societies and conserve natural resources. For instance, Abu Baker Alsiddique (the first caliph) gave the following Ten Commandments to Yazid Ibn Abu Sufyan, one of his army leaders: 'Do not kill a woman, a child or an old person. Do not cut a fruit tree, or destroy buildings. Do not kill a goat or a camel except for a meal. Do not burn palm trees, or flood them. Do not betray and do not spread panic' (Al-Tamimi, 2003).

Part 4: Application

THE ROYAL SOCIETY FOR THE CONSERVATION OF NATURE (RSCN)

Chapter 10 presents first case study. The RSCN began to implement all the elements and governing rules of I.Theory, providing me with an opportunity to monitor and test the theory on the ground and to see how the RSCN could use it to achieve a new management orientation and transcendent quality. From there, I launched I.Theory in its entirety, through my meetings as a co-researcher with the co-operative inquiry teams of researchers at RSCN.

Through my application of I.Theory at RSCN, we began to transform towards a *'Beit al-Hikma'* (House of Wisdom) (Khaled, 2005). RSCN, then, has adopted an Islamic knowledge perspective and has begun, or at least attempted, to implement the justice value amongst its employees. What sort of difficulties did it face during this transitional period? How will managers and employees accept this radical change? What will emerge from it, as far as an Islamic approach to quality and sustainability is concerned? How do the systems of I.Theory work in practice – specifically in the context of an organisation working with nature and with close-knit rural, Bedouin communities?

What is it that I am testing overall? I am reviewing and testing quality and transformation. Through my role in management consulting, my norms are propelling me to implement and help to create standards to achieve quality (*Itqan*) in Islam, and transformation development, and to promote them through management by values.

However, from the beginning, the transformation process appeared to emanate from an initial change in the top management, when Yehya Khaled was appointed Acting Director General, after having lived through the preceding transformation process at RSCN and undergone the master's course in Transformation Management at Buckingham University.

AL-QUDS PAINTS CO.

In Chapter 11, I build up the second case study, of Al-Quds Paints Co., a private enterprise where I have had a second opportunity to implement I.Theory and build human resource (HR) systems. I started with a co-operative inquiry team headed by the general manager, Amer Jubran, who was introduced to the world of paints at the age of 10, during the school summer holidays of 1983. The factory's journey is a story of blood, sweat and tears and ultimate success. During my work with Amer Jubran and the co-operative team, he was highly committed to implementing the values-managed organisation concepts based on Islamic values, and gave all his attention to the cultural change that took place with the implementation of the systems that we built together. He started applying all the principles required to create a values-managed organisation, with some special emphasis on knowledge sharing, codes of ethics, evaluation processes and the learning organisation. As we shall see, there were at least four main types of inquiry outcome, corresponding to the four types of knowing: experiential, presentational, propositional and practical.

The co-operative inquiry methodology required the collaborative participation of key members of RSCN and Al-Quds Paints Co., together with me. We worked with case methods to test the assumptions built into the I.Theory, in order to evolve them accordingly, and ultimately to develop the two organisations towards quality and transformation.

Part 5: Conclusions

Chapter 12 reflects my conclusions. I have tried to re-visit quality and transformation from the perspectives of I.Theory and of the absence of justice and will in our countries, in addition to future implications and my future role.

To conclude, through the implementation of systems based on I.Theory we have sown the seeds of a new local–global quality of working life. However, identifying the results will be part of my continuing work on other consultancy-based assignments involving other Jordanian enterprises in the private sector.

I will now proceed to the first part of this book and the story of myself, my organisation and my society that provides a backdrop to the burning issues we are addressing as the Arab Awakening takes place around us, at least in my consultancy-based case, from an Arab institutional perspective.

2 The Origin of the Transformation: Our Stories

My Own Story

SELF, ORGANISATION AND SOCIETY

In the first chapter, I provided an overview of the book as a whole, its context and orientation, the methodological approach, the underlying theory, and the subsequent applications of I.Theory. This chapter covers our stories, as myself, organisation and society, starting with my own story, to set the context.

My story evolves from my birth in Palestine to my present life in Jordan, and includes the different situations in my life as a Muslim and an Arab that have affected my views on quality of work and life and triggered my interest in quality and transformation. I will cover my work in education, which spanned 15 years and covered Yemen, Libya, Algeria and Jordan. I will also discuss my organisation, TEAM International, and its ground-breaking work in Jordan and the region in relation to quality and quality management systems. I will end by discussing the economy and society of Jordan, its different elements and shortcomings, pin-pointing the need for quality and transformation in all sectors of life and exploring a state-run programme for socio-economic transformation.

LIFE AND CAREER PATH

I was born into a Palestinian family in a small Palestinian town in 1947, a catastrophic year for the Palestinian people, and for many Arabs and Muslims, and a very challenging historical moment for everybody living there at that time. The conflict between Arabs and the Zionist movement was raging, and led to the war of 1948 and the establishment of the State of Israel. The war resulted in floods of Palestinian refugees entering neighbouring Arab countries, especially Transjordan, where my family ended up. This was a very early, and allegedly traumatic, period of my life. I was 6 months old.

At the time, my family consisted of my parents and their six sons and three daughters. Due to the family's limited financial means, my brothers left school at an early age and went to work to support our family. However, appreciating the significance of education for stateless people, my parents insisted that the girls in the family should complete their education.

I completed my preparatory and secondary education in Amman, Jordan. As early as the elementary period, I started to think about economics, encouraged by my father's immortal saying 'Save your penny for a rainy day'. He said it differently though: 'Save your white piaster for a black day'. Maybe both sayings accurately describe our days then, since rainy and dark days were the harsh realities we had to face. He always quoted the holy Qur'an, asking people to avoid waste in every way possible, such as *aya* (verse) 141 in *sura* Al-An'am (the Cattle):[1] *'But waste not by excess: for Allah loveth not the wasters.'* And when he wanted to remind us of the need to save, he reminded us of what Allah says in this regard: *'Verily, all things have we created by measure'*, *'Everything to him is measured'*, and *'And we have produced therein everything in balance'* (*sura* Al-Qamar [the Moon], *aya* 49). This was the early foundation for my subsequent pursuit of quality.

I received my general certificate of secondary education in 1965. For my degree, I attended Jordan University. I majored in economics, hoping that one day I would become minister of planning so that I might implement development plans for the lagging Jordanian economy and maybe transform and advance the country. I graduated in 1969 with a bachelor's degree in Economics and Statistics. During my time at university, the Arab–Israeli war of 1967 erupted and yet more Palestinian refugees flooded into Jordan. This negatively affected the employment situation in the country.

I did not therefore have a chance to work in Jordan. Instead, I was lucky to be able to sign up for a work contract with UNESCO to work in Yemen as a lecturer in household economics. That was during the period 1970–1971. Yemen then was the most poverty-stricken and least developed of the Arab countries. It needed a great deal of effort just to survive, never mind to develop. So I decided to work hard for the people of that country, to help in the development process there.

My belief was that Yemen should be developed through the efforts of its people and of others who could make sincere efforts along such lines. I worked as a teacher in the only girls' school at that time, in the capital, San'aa. I became involved in the formal and informal education of the girls, the latter through fruitful relationships with their families. It was a starting-point for identifying gender indicators such as population composition and change, households and families, marital status and fertility, economic activity and labour-force participation against poverty.

At the same time, I started voluntary work at the radio station to educate Yemeni families, particularly the women and girls. The programme was broadcast twice a week and was a success during the whole of my contract period. Following that, I left Yemen for Libya, where I was appointed in 1972 as a teacher of economics and statistics at one of the Social Service Institutes for girls. Girls were more educated in Libya than in Yemen. They developed many skills, particularly in the social arena, and had good opportunities to focus on human development generally and on women's issues in particular.

Compared to Yemen, Libya was considered more developed. The capital, Tripoli, was more modern than San'aa. I liked my work in the institute, working with 18-year-old girls. One reason why I focused on these girls was my belief that the core of the development process lies with women, and that it is they who can help to establish the sustainability and development, as well as the competence, that youths in the Arab world needed most. Women needed to play a big role in Arab and Muslim societies, especially given their

---

1   I will alternate between three translations of the Holy Qur'an in order to use the translation that best conveys the meaning because some of the translations contain mistakes or are not clear. The selection is by no means arbitrary and is based on a thorough comparison between three translations: (1) *The Qur'an, A New Translation* by Thomas Cleary; (2) *Al-Qur'an, A Contemporary Translation* by Ahmed Ali; and (3) *Roman Translation of the Holy Qur'an* by Abdullah Yusuf Ali.

family and social responsibilities, such as their roles in raising their children and in the conservation of resources.

I felt that my work was not of a traditional kind, but a sort of responsibility towards achieving a renaissance of Arab societies and the advancement of awareness of women's role in social development. The situation of Arab and Muslim women was affected by the patriarchal nature of Islamic society. For long periods of time, women were subjected to injustice and oppression by men and society. Many years later, I met some of my past students. Some had assumed very good positions in government ministries in Yemen and Libya, and this was a source of pride for me in my work.

Returning afterwards to Jordan, I found a job at the Arab Bank, where I was assigned to the deposits section. The manager refused to give me a more responsible job, one having to do with the bank policies, because at that time important positions were assigned only to men. The justification for this was that women tended to quit work after marriage to raise their families.

Transforming Mental Models

At that time, I got married and moved to Algeria with my husband. In Algeria a new phase began in my life, with new challenges for me to tackle. I needed to learn French so as to be able to deal with people, as well as with official organisations. By going to France for two months to learn the language at its source, so to speak, I succeeded in learning the language very quickly. After that language drill, I returned to Algeria more able to deal with people and pursue my personal and work life without any fear of being excluded by a language barrier. One of my achievements was successfully teaching Algerian Arab elementary teachers how to teach in Arabic.

I lived in Algeria for five years. It was a tough place to live and work at that time, especially in the field of education. But that was part of my lot in life and a reflection of my circumstances as an Arab person helping Arab people to develop, roaming the Arab world and shouldering my share of responsibility.

At the end of that period I lost my first child, at the age of three, in an accident. I understood that death and life are unified like river and sea: death is the freedom of the soul to join its Creator. It was an event that showed me the cycle of life, and a key factor in changing my life and making me ponder again the questions 'Why do we live? And how do we leave a legacy in this short life?' I decided, as a result, to return to Jordan. It was eight years since I had last been there. I started a job as a lecturer in a community college and stayed there for six years (1978–1984), teaching and learning economics, managerial sciences and finance.

By the end of that period, I had worked as a teacher for about 15 years. I found that teaching required new mental models, and this required me to be a learner as well as an educator. Teaching also requires deep debate about normative, ethical and spiritual issues. All these norms are based on mastery (*Itqan*) in Islam. There is also an emphasis on the quality of performance. Islam invites believers to aspire to perfection in their deeds, and to be kind and merciful to other creatures. It was stated by the Prophet Mohammad that '*Allah loves to see one's job done at the level of Itqan*'. All this made me wonder why my fellow Muslims, in business specifically, if not in life generally, did not pay more attention to such guidance.

My work in Jordan from 1978 to 1984 as a lecturer and freelance consultant conducting feasibility studies helped me to familiarise myself with the Jordanian market and recognise the different managerial styles used in conducting business. I experienced different organisations and their attitudes to development both positively and negatively. Eventually, I succeeded in representing TEAM International in Jordan. This included opening a branch to start a development and management consulting business.

ENTERING INTO MANAGEMENT CONSULTANCY

Often, managers learn to improve organisational performance, quality and transformation through their experience of other managers and business organisations. Management consulting is a useful professional service that gives managers an alternative means to analyse and solve the problems facing their organisations.

I thought that by developing and establishing management consulting and training services for various sectors of the economy I could achieve my goals in the area of sustainability and development. What I subsequently realised, and as this book will reveal, my efforts were at best only partially successful, because I was not yet aware of the factors determining business development in our region. Yet it was a great opportunity for me to implement my beliefs and ideas – such as they were at the time – about organisational and transformational development.

I saw management consulting as a dynamic and rapidly changing sector of professional services, aimed at improving human behaviour in organisations and building a people-centred identity for organisations in the Arab world. It was relevant and useful to clients. At the same time, consultants need to keep abreast of economic and social trends. They should be ready to provide the advice that clients seek in order to achieve and maintain high performance. This kind of service fitted in with my objectives and principles for enhancing the value of the service provided by TEAM as a consulting firm. It was an extension of the adult education in which I had been extensively involved, especially when TEAM International provided a development service for women,[2] through a special training centre based on Arab culture, leading to sustainability at a macroeconomic level. That was my hope.

Actually, however, the consulting assignments lasted for too short a time, and predominantly Western concepts were applied to local Arab contexts. I began to expand my horizons, ultimately towards business development arising from local identity and evolving towards global integrity. Such transformation within an organisation – indeed like TEAM's, as we shall see – while drawing upon global methods, would need to be based on local culture. I now turn from self and organisation, from my Arab and Islamic background, to quality and transformation.

2　Such as project management and how a woman can start a project to generate income, in addition to problem solving, decision making and how to benefit from these managerial skills in her life generally, and to sustain her family specifically.

The Story of TEAM: Transport, Engineering and Management

THE BIRTH AND GROWTH OF TEAM INTERNATIONAL

TEAM International was established in Lebanon in 1975 and moved its headquarters to Cairo in 1976. The founders were university professors working in the American University in Beirut, teaching engineering and management sciences. They believed in the importance of developing the Arab world and recognised the need for a local Arab consulting firm offering consultancy services ostensibly based on Arab and local culture.

The founders of TEAM saw an opportunity in the markets of the Middle East, to offer a service in accordance with local needs, and to be sustainable.

The establishment of the first TEAM office in Beirut was followed a year later by the opening of another office, in Cairo. The two capitals were selected for TEAM's activities on the basis of market demand, which was focused on management consultancy. The oil-rich Gulf States, led mainly by Saudi Arabia, provided big opportunities as clients of TEAM International. Saudi Arabia had an urgent need for infrastructure, urban planning and transportation and project management.

Another branch, in Riyadh, was opened in 1975, and several projects were carried out.

TEAM International's mission was 'developing organisations with the purpose of improving productivity and efficiency, exploring or pursuing new business opportunities, and training individuals at all management levels, which is to be seen to reflect the needs of the organisation and the community as a whole'.

Actually, TEAM's focus has mainly been on training and management consulting in Arab organisations, using 'Western' techniques and technologies, and this has led to modernising processes. Trainees were subsequently promoted to better work opportunities and to developing the organisations. As market demand increased, TEAM International expanded its operations to more Arab countries. By the mid-1980s, TEAM had established 14 branches in the Arab world. The company's headquarters were ultimately based in Cairo, and five major centres were established:

- Management Consulting Centre
- Systems Technology Centre
- Engineering Consulting Centre
- Arab Centre for Educational and Social (including Women's) Development
- Arab Centre for Management Development.

With the first three centres, TEAM left a mark on many Arab organisations in Lebanon, Saudi Arabia and in all the Arabian Gulf Emirates in the 1970s and 1980s. It also played an outstanding role in Algeria with the Arab Centre for Educational and Social Development, spreading and helping people to (re-)learn the Arabic language, with a special focus on women's development, after the country gained its independence from France.

As a part of its Educational and Social Development mission, TEAM International used the company's centres around the region to establish the first Arab computer camps during the period 1985–95. The idea behind these camps was to spread information technology (IT) among youngsters aged 8 to 16 and to establish a future clientele for the company. These camps brought Arab children from everywhere in the Arab world and beyond to receive appropriate computer training, have fun, build team spirit and spread cultural awareness. The computer camps, supervised by TEAM staff, created a positive spirit and helped the youths attending these camps to develop into mature and responsible adults.

I supervised and managed these computer camps for three consecutive years. Many youths of both sexes who attended the camps later became IT managers. It was a step in the right direction, towards building competence, personality and organisational thinking. More importantly, it was an unplanned step towards sustaining a business–consumer relationship, but one that was not progressively built upon on a long-term basis.

In the 1990s TEAM International embarked on a new management educational venture, together with City University Business School in the UK.

FROM CONSULTING TO MANAGEMENT DEVELOPMENT

Long-term management development programmes were initiated in 1992, when TEAM started promoting long-term management development and organisational learning. This was done through the Management Masters of Business Administration degree (MMBA), which the City University of London offered in the Middle East jointly with TEAM International for the purpose of developing the business environment. A number of courses were offered that led to an MMBA. It was not, at the time, a transformation programme, but merely a continuation of the professionalising agenda. There was no regional or Islamic context to the programme and no sustainability was built into it. It was a 'Westernised', degree-based programme. I could see that it at least held more promise, however, than the outmoded programmes in the Arab world. However, after six years of its operation, now lacking institutional support at City University Business School for the programme's product champion (who had put his heart and soul into it), the university terminated the programme because it appeared not to be commercially viable. In fact, it had taken off in Jordan, in the West Bank and Gaza, and to some extent in the Lebanon, but not in Egypt.

TEAM International, meanwhile, carried out a large number of projects in management and engineering in a wide range of Arab countries. Over a quarter of a century, its programmes supported governments, institutions and companies and helped them to face the challenges of change and development. These programmes served to develop a clear vision, steady improvement, employee empowerment and dedication to customer satisfaction. TEAM continues to act as an effective vehicle for the transfer and application of the latest global advances in management, engineering, IT and HR development, and to deliver high-quality services to its clients in the Arab region.

In TEAM Jordan, of which I was the founder and am currently the General Manager, we took the initiative to develop management consultancy services in Jordan and to extend the service to other centres in Cairo, Egypt and Riyadh/Saudi Arabia, with a view to ultimately – unlike our TEAM International colleagues – taking into consideration the cultural context, core values and codes of ethics.

THE ORIGIN OF QUALITY IN TEAM/JORDAN

A branch of TEAM was established in Jordan in 1988. It was decided to start our consulting business on both an individual and an organisational level by using multi-theme-based training, serving especially the banking community and industrial organisations. TEAM Jordan's rapid growth in its early years was aided by a lack of competition. At that time, traditional management approaches were dominant in the Jordanian market, accompanied by lagging international management standards. In other words, either parochial, all-too-often dysfunctional, approaches prevailed, or else the global dominated the local, with nothing local–global in between. If the truth be told, though, at that stage in my individual and organisational development we were not thinking in such terms.

By 1991, TEAM Jordan was beginning to focus on management consulting in the areas of organisational structure, job description, feasibility studies and investment analysis. We progressively gained confidence, with the support and backing of TEAM International. Shared resources included regional projects and activities executed and signed by TEAM International in many Arab, and also African, countries. But this was traditional management and engineering consultancy. I began to think about how to develop our work more sustainably, based on our Islamic knowledge and indigenous culture, as well as drawing on exogenous knowledge. So, in 1995 TEAM Jordan started offering quality management systems (QMS) for different industrial and service sectors. We had an advantage over our competitors in the Jordanian market because of our strong market share, in general, and our quality-oriented activities, in particular. At that stage, in the mid-1990s, we were drawing on a global 'Western' orientation to QMS, with some local adaptations, but that was all. More integral development was yet to come, a decade or so later.

In fact, at TEAM Jordan we found that total quality needs to be viewed as one system that integrates both the managerial and the technical systems. Building a total quality (TQ) organisation necessitates a review of systems and the development of a culture that provides the motivation and direction for everyone to work towards the organisation's vision. It requires an understanding of how organisations learn and sustain themselves in order to serve their communities.

I began to realise that pursuing quality is a journey. It is an important tool for organisational transformation, and for community transformation as well.

The expansion of TQM and QMS benefited TEAM Jordan as well as other TEAM International branches in different Arab countries, from Egypt to Lebanon, from the West Bank to Morocco, from Saudi Arabia to Yemen. The international office in Cairo supported TEAM Jordan's objectives in resource and human development as well as in developing new products. However, our initial approach to TQM, throughout the Arab region, was very much influenced by global TQ and International Organization for Standardization (ISO) exogenous standards, and did not explicitly incorporate indigenous knowledge.

In other words, at that time we were relating a 'global' quality approach to local culture, rather than evolving the global out of the local (Lessem, and Schieffer 2009). At the same time, as we were endogenously aware, Allah (God) encouraged people who accomplished good work: 'And gladden those who believe and do good works, with the news that there are gardens for them, beneath which rivers flow' (sura Al-Baqarah [the Cow], aya 25). Allah also said: 'And as for those who believe and do good works, God will pay them their rewards. And God does not love wrong doers' (sura Al-Imran [the Family of Imran], aya 57).

Thus, when we in TEAM Jordan explicitly affirmed that good business documentation is basic for building a global quality system, we were implicitly confirming what the Almighty ordered us to do: that is, to be open and clear in our business dealings with each other. Moreover, since the primary goal of applying the global quality system is for every employee in the institution to do his and her job as it should be done, we reflected by that what the Prophet Mohammad confirms in his teachings: *'Allah loves to see one's job done at the level of itqan.'* TEAM experts were able to integrate international quality standards through these easy-to-apply local culture measures, and to make quality work part and parcel of work ethics and social responsibility.

TEAM Jordan was a pioneer as a consulting firm in QMS in this part of the Arab world. It helped over 300 organisations to obtain quality certificates, leading to the realisation of one aspect of organisational sustainability: clear and relevant documentation. However, continuing transformation depends on actual implementation and continual improvement, and the evolution of local identity towards global integrity. More of that, as we shall see, was yet to come. My and our transformational journey was yet to be completed.

Transformation, moreover, was not for organisations only, but for society as a whole. So I extended my work to protecting and conserving our society by applying the Environmental Management System (EMS ISO 14001), version 1996. It was not surprising, given the way my thinking was evolving, indigenously as well as exogenously, to find that the requirements of ISO 14001 were mentioned in Islam – for example, urging Muslims to avoid whatever threatens life. Pollution is a very serious threat; it may turn one's life into misery. Not only does it threaten mankind, it also threatens livestock, agriculture, water and industry. Prophet Mohammad (Peace be upon him) urged Muslims to practise agriculture; he is quoted as saying, *'If a Muslim cultivates a piece of land, he should claim its property'* (Al-Tamimi, 2003).

However, those specific references to Islam were not enough; not for me, anyway. I was beginning to find it necessary to look for an overall consulting, local–global evolution, that is, to transform all the activities in any organisation on the basis of indigenous values that urge people to do their best. At that time, in 2003, I met an unusual Jordanian management academic, Dr Assaf. He was, unusually for that time, not willing to submit entirely to 'Western' management ideas. We discussed how we might channel management consultancy to serve our organisations and our society, indigenously as well as exogenously. He indicated that he was in the process of writing a theory of management based on Islamic culture, which he called I.Theory/Management by Values – the 'I' standing for Islamic. I realised that he was really on to something, and was keen to collaborate with him.

BUILDING TEAM'S CODE OF ETHICS

During my leadership of TEAM Jordan (which is still in place), we maintained a code of ethics based on honesty and professionalism, even during the most difficult times. This code is rooted in deeply held religious beliefs that are well established in our region. Quality performance equates to what we call in Arabic *'Itqan'* (perfection), something that should be a way of life for truly devout Muslims. The code of ethics that we have in TEAM Jordan is our guide in performing our work; and we ask new recruits to TEAM to adhere to it.

As a further development in the field of HR development (within the context of sustainability and continuity), in 2001 we formed a new partnership between TEAM Jordan and the University of Buckingham, UK, to where the former product champion from City University had now moved. We were to share in the development and promotion of an MSc degree in Transformation Management, directed primarily towards managers in business, as a further step in the transformation of individuals, organisations and societies towards sustainable development. The agreement was signed in 2001, resulting in a two-year part-time programme that was in fact a further evolution of the City University-based MMBA, now offering a master's degree in Transformation Management aimed mostly at senior managers involved in the development of their sponsoring organisations. There were four parties involved: TEAM, University of Buckingham, the newly evolving TRANS4M (Geneva) as a Centre for Social Innovation, and the participating organisations. The degree was aimed at promoting sustainable – in the sense of combining indigenous wisdom with exogenous knowledge – development through organisational learning and knowledge creation.

Whilst development is a force for change, sustainability is a force for continuity. Taking into consideration both nature and culture, from both physical and human perspectives the programme was ultimately aimed at promoting societal transformation locally, within a global context. The programme concentrated on enterprise and governance, and on culture and community in the process of transformation. Participants in the programme included the Vice Chairman of Middle East Complex, the largest industrial company in the region; the prospective Managing Director of the RSCN, which became one of my case applications of I.Theory; the principal of Ahlliyah International School for Girls; and two managers from King Abdullah II Design and Development Bureau, all working towards transformation management. We also had many successful organisations that were trying to build a new culture to improve their productivity towards sustainability and transformation, such as National Paints and Dar Al-Dawa pharmaceutical company.

On a personal level, I received my MSc degree in Transformation Management in 2003 and proceeded soon afterwards to my doctoral programme in socio-economic transformation. Some of the course work for this programme was applied within my organisation and in Jordanian society as part of an emerging transformation process. Moreover, we in TEAM Jordan were determined to develop and apply this new management model, which comes from our religion and local culture, in the Arab region.

Through my professional development in TEAM, overall, then, I could trace a path from productivity to quality and from quality to transformation, with local as well as global overtones. In the next section I turn to society and societal transformation within Jordan, to highlight the setting of our work in society at large.

The Story of Jordan, My Society

JORDAN – A SMALL COUNTRY

Jordan is a small country in the Middle East. Its people are of mixed origins and a unique alignment has been established between them in order to achieve social development. This is especially important because Jordan is poor in natural resources such as forests, coal reserves, hydroelectric power or commercially viable oil deposits. Moreover, being a small economy with limited natural resources and a small market makes Jordan sensitive to regional changes and global conditions. Thus, the performance of the Jordanian economy suffers noticeably from the adverse effects of unfavourable regional conditions.

As a result of all of the above, there has been a growing need for wide-ranging participation in the process of development, one that will ultimately enable all Jordanians to participate in building their country so as to accelerate social and economic development. The government of Jordan started its so called 'transformation' programme with that end in mind six years ago, in association with the World Bank and the International Monetary Fund (IMF).

WORLD BANK-INSTIGATED EXOGENOUS TRANSFORMATION

The Jordanian government's transformation programme, instigated globally by the World Bank rather than locally–globally in I.Theory terms, was aimed at achieving modernisation, and not authentic indigenous–exogenous development, from our perspective. It involved a change from the traditional, parochial approach used in past years for economic and social development, which did not provide measurable results and was supposedly not geared towards sustainable development. The problem, as I have now intimated, was that the focus of this transformation programme was exclusively on physical infrastructure: buildings, roads, bridges and other infrastructure. That was a good thing, to an extent, but we needed to bring about a transformation in people's mentalities. We needed to help them to evolve and transform themselves, their organisations and their community.

Currently, the Ministry of Planning and International Cooperation directs this programme on behalf of the government of Jordan. The following objectives are being addressed (www.mop.gov.jo):

- Completion of plans of action according to timetables set for all projects covered by the programme.
- Production of monthly and annual cash flows of the programme. These were distributed to ministries and all governorates in the kingdom. In addition, estimates of the economic categorisation of programme expenditures for current and capital expenses, as well as distribution of expenditures on the local market and imports, are all presented.
- Building a model to set priorities, starting with projects that will have a direct impact on people's living conditions. A number of factors were defined to set criteria for priorities to be implemented. These include: unemployment, poverty, geographical distribution of projects across different governorates, allocating some of the programme's money to local markets and to imports, classification of the programme expenditures between current expenditure and capital expenditure, etc.
- Intensification of efforts with donors and creditors to provide funding for the transformation programme, coupled with persistent and intensive support from His Majesty King Abdullah II for programmed implementation.
- Tying programmed implementation to decentralisation of policies and development so that different governorates plan, finance and implement programmes enhancing the drive towards sustainable development.
- Setting legislative guidelines that have been or will be amended or issued under the socio-economic transformation programme.

- Undertaking evaluative studies, in association with the World Bank, on the programme's impact on economic growth, poverty and unemployment as well as other related social and economic factors.
- Monitoring projects and procedures included in the programme components with its public and private investment details, organisational control, institutional and legislative framework, and policies.
- Completion of the programme's draft budget for the fiscal year 2003 in co-ordination and consultation with all concerned parties.

The programme is probably typical of such globally initiated World Bank activities, focused on technological and economic development to the exclusion of local culture and spirit. After six years, the government, unsurprisingly, is still not achieving the above-mentioned objectives and has been asked to undertake a management review of this programme to see why it has not achieved the required results. From my perspective, in response to this situation, to begin with, real transformation needs to take place in the people's mental and emotional orientation and in human development. It needs to start from the ground up and have a direct impact on people in order to achieve a radical change. The economic and technological perspective by itself does not do enough to build transformation into society at large. By way of contrast, the transformation management programme that we worked with in co-operation with the University of Buckingham and TRANS4M dealt directly with the transformation of the self, organisation and society. Ironically, the programme was closed down in 2005 because we could not secure local accreditation from those very bodies that were championing the orthodox approach to technological–economic transformation identified above.

Meanwhile, I never lost my focus on the involvement of women in transformation, because of women's impact on their families and the coming generations. When TEAM started the computer camps programme for Arab youth in the 1980s, with which I was directly involved, it started to build a technology base in the region. In that context, the feminine (women's energy and orientation) and the masculine (technology) could meet.

Conclusion

According to Jordan's Department of Statistics, the total number of economic establishments in Jordan in 2003 exceeded 210,000. Their paid-up capital exceeded (Jordanian dollars) JD5.7 billion, while the gross investment was much higher until 2000. Residents contributed 72 per cent of the paid-up capital of these establishments, while the share of non-resident investors was 15 per cent and the government's share, including that of ministries and other departments, was 13 per cent (Jordan Economy, website).

The majority of Jordanian business organisations (JBOs) were established during the 1970s and 1980s, following the oil boom in the mid-1970s and the subsequent major political developments in the region, including the Lebanese civil war and the first Gulf War. The publicly quoted companies constitute not more than 20 per cent of the total employment in Jordan's private sector.

Features of the management and organisation of JBOs are:

1. Lack of delegation of authority

2. Lack of an elaborated organisational structure, lower status of personnel departments
3. Lack of systems and regulations – no vision or clear mission
4. Lack of professional relations between managers (Al-Rasheed, 2001).

We would argue that this is due, above all, to the lack of any explicitly home-grown management theory and practice analogous to, for example, 'Japanese spirit/Western technique' management, which evolved from the 1950s to the early 1990s in Japan. That said, there is a largely shared Jordanian culture with distinct social, historical and developmental features. However, and this applies throughout the Arab world, a purposeful link between tradition and modernity has not been devised, which is one of the reasons why an 'Arab Awakening' is occurring only now.

Therefore we need an indigenous–exogenous transformation management model to develop business in Jordan and in the region. The model needs to be linked with the development of human beings based on their culture and nature, serving to bridge the gap between the local and the global, the indigenous and the exogenous, tradition and modernity, culture and economy, so as to achieve overall effectiveness. Specifically, in effect, in its pursuit of quality and transformation the model needs to integrate the Arab and Islamic heritage with a global orientation. This needs a transformation of thought and practice. With this end in mind, I will turn later to my methodology, or approach to local–global knowledge creation. Before doing so, however, I need to present the consulting practice in which I am involved.

3 *Management Consulting as a Path to Quality and Transformation*

Introduction

MY CONSULTING JOURNEY: OUTSIDE-IN TO INSIDE-OUT

In my own life and work journey, as you will by now know, in Palestine and in Jordan, in Algeria and in Yemen, in Egypt and back to Jordan, I have been continually engaged in enabling my fellow Arabs to develop, most specifically within the arenas of business and the economy. The particular medium in which I have been engaged for the past three decades or so has been in management 'consultancy', or *al Shura* to use Islamic and Arabic terms. While this consultancy started out, for me at least, as a globally instigated, 'Western' pursuit, I have never lost touch with my Arabic and Muslim roots, and in my consultancy practice in recent years I have begun to work with these explicitly, , ultimately though I.Theory. I begin this chapter, however, with a description of the nature and scope of my consultancy practice, which has been with TEAM from the outset.

It is through my career a as management consultant that I have played an important part in applying quality and transformation in organisations, initially globally–locally, and more recently locally–globally. During my career of 25 years in developing and sustaining organisations in Jordan and in Arab countries, my role a as management consultant has given me the confidence to work with top management and to implement management systems to develop and improve organisations.

In the process, as a management consultant in Jordan I have engaged specifically with privatisation, e-government and TQM – in addition to TEAM's role generally in promoting TQM and transformation management – by qualifying companies and organisations to achieve the King Abdullah II Award for Excellence. Having first studied and applied endogenous approaches in our indigenous context, I then turned my profession inside out, locally–globally, through I.Theory, as we shall see later in this book. I adopted this Islamic approach to quality and to quality of life at the level of the self, the organisation and society.

So what is the management consulting profession with which I have been engaged? This chapter covers different definitions of management consulting, from different points of view. It also focuses on the Arab context, alongside management consulting as a profession, with the *Mustashar* (counsellor or advisor), *Shura* (consultation) and *Ijma* (consensus) as basic and essential values in Muslim society. I start with definitions. This chapter also covers the consultation processes, such as problem solving, identifying new opportunities, enhancing learning and implementing change to create transformational organisations. We will start with origins.

ORIGINS: THE WEST DOMINATES THE REST

Management consulting is a method for improving management practices and achieving organisational transformation. Generally speaking, it is globally conceived, specifically in the Anglo-Saxon 'West', while also being locally applied, as has been the case in Jordan. An independent organisation or internal consulting unit in public or private organisations can use this consulting approach. At the same time, management consulting has been developing as a profession. Thousands of individuals and their organisations practise consulting and strive to achieve professional standards related to the quality of the advice provided, methods of intervention and ethical principles – again, all of these having been conceived of in the 'West', albeit with local adaptations to 'the rest'.

Consulting thus has two aspects: consulting as a method and consulting as a profession. There is no conflict between the two, as they both work towards achieving the objectives of both the consultants and the clients on the road to improving and transforming their organisations towards quality and effectiveness – invariably as exogenously derived and conceived. The origin of management consulting lies in the Industrial Revolution in England, the advent of the modern factory and the related institutional and social transformations, and specifically 'work study' practices of 'scientific management', that brought it about. The contemporary theory and modern practice are predominantly American, rather than British, in origin, with international consultancy firms like McKinsey and Accenture ruling the roost – the latter, like several others, being an offshoot of an accounting practice. Their 'Western' roots, as such, are identical with those of management as a distinct area of human activity and a field of learning. In that context, methodologically and ontologically, these firms are characteristically 'positivist', that is, they are supposedly 'value free' in orientation. This 'consulting' theory and practice, moreover, are based on a view of reality in which an 'objective observer' can analyse organisational phenomena, thereby being externally 'consulted', and then leave the internal implementation of the consultant's findings to the organisation itself – which of course bears the consequences!

THE INFLUENCE OF 'SCIENTIFIC' MANAGEMENT

Such 'scientific management' pioneers as America's Frederick W. Taylor, Frank and Lillian Gilbert, Gant and Emerson, gave major impetus to the initial development of management consultancy. In their technical and instrumentalist approaches to simplifying work processes and raising the productivity of workers (as 'objects') and plant, they all believed in the application of an objectively 'scientific' (without regard to the workers' culture, spirit or subjectivity) method to the solution of production problems. They focused mainly on factory and shop-floor productivity and efficiency, rational work organisation, time and motion study, with a view to eliminating waste and reducing production costs. The management philosophy emphasised tasks, to the exclusion of a more humanistic orientation, and the approach was universalist and standardised, without taking into account the inevitable cultural – that is American – bias.

This specific area of management was given the name 'industrial engineering'. The practitioners, called 'efficiency experts', were admired for their drive, their methodical approach and the improvements they achieved. The early image of such management consultants has changed somewhat, over the years, because new areas of management and new types of problems have been tackled and have become a normal part of the consulting business. However, consultants continue to be regarded as people to find new opportunities for saving resources and raising productivity, even where others see none.

FREEDOM, EQUALITY AND JUSTICE

Management consulting generally, then, and total quality specifically, as we shall see, reflects the general intellectual and societal – in this case predominantly 'Western' – philosophy of an age. However, in the terms to be articulated in this book, management consultancy, from a broader, more culturally differentiated perspective, will reflect the individual 'freedom' embedded in a Western approach, the social 'equality' embodied in the Japanese one and, finally, and most importantly for our purposes here, as evolved through this book, the 'justice' value embodied in I.Theory. We now turn to definitions of management consultancy from, respectively, 'Western' and Islamic perspectives (the latter further evolved in this book), starting with the former.

The Conventional Exogenous Wisdom on Consultancy

FUNCTIONAL AND PROFESSIONAL

I now want to compare and contrast the conventional, global approach with the unconventional, Arab and Islamic approach to consultancy. There are, conventionally speaking to begin with, many definitions of management consultancy and its applications to management situations and problems. However, two basic approaches predominate. The first takes a broad functional view of consulting. Fritz Steele defines it in this way: 'By the consulting process, I mean any form providing help on the content, process or structure of a task or series of tasks, where the consultant is not actually responsible for doing the task itself but is helping those who are' (Steel, 1975). Peter Block suggests that 'You are consulting any time you are trying to change or to improve a situation but have no direct control over the implementation. Most people in staff roles in organisations are really consultants even if they don't officially call themselves that' (Block, 1981). That means that consultants are helpers or enablers, and assumes that such help can be provided by persons doing different jobs.

The second approach views consulting as a special professional service and emphasises a number of characteristics. According to Larry Greiner and Robert Metzger: 'Management consulting is an advisory service contracted for and provided to organisations by specially trained and qualified persons who assist, in an objective and independent manner, the client organisation to identify management problems, analyse such problems, recommend solutions to these problems, and help, when requested, in the implementation of solutions' (Greiner and Metzger, 1983).

For Kuber (1996), who regards the two approaches as complementary rather than conflicting, management consulting can be viewed either as a professional service or as a method of providing practical advice and help. He writes: 'There is no doubt that management consulting has been developing into a specific sector of professional activity and should be treated as such. At the same time, it is also a method of assisting organisations and executives in improving management and business practices, as well as individual and organisational performance.'

Similar or less detailed definitions are used by other authors, such as Dahlan Abdullah: 'It is an activity by individual, firm or association based on the study of any problem and applying its solution to achieve improvement or development.' He adds: 'The core of the consulting work is thought. It is a thinking process towards the confirmation of any work performed with a large quantity of effectiveness to achieve the best results' (Abu Sheikha, 1986). There is no great difference between these definitions; but for me, as a consultant, all definitions are encompassed in the following:

1. Management consulting is a professional service, whether providing technical knowledge or skills related to practical management or business problems. The accumulation of experience and knowledge from different situations, combined with the skills needed for solving problems, improves organisational performance. This is achieved by sharing experiences with others, understanding the nature and goals of organisations, finding and analysing information, coping with resistance to change, motivating people, and so on. Thus, consulting can be an essential experience for organisational transformation such as: operations research, systems theories, computer science and information technology, behavioural sciences and other scientific investigations into the functioning and behaviour of human organisations and systems in the business and social sectors.
2. Management consulting is an independent service; the consultant does not accept any information or suggestions based on the client's opinion, nor does he make biased assessment of any situation that might affect his own interests. He must build his own conclusions, objectively, for this is what the client's organisation needs. The prime purpose of management consulting is to help enterprises to adopt appropriate strategies to achieve intra-organisational and inter-organisational transformation.
3. Management consulting is an advisory service; the consultant is not used to run an organisation or to make decisions on behalf of the managers. While maintaining quality and integrity, it is his responsibility to provide advice, without any authority to decide on the changes and their final implementation.

VARIATIONS ON A CONVENTIONAL CONSULTANCY THEME

For Kuber, then, the purposes of consulting can be viewed from several angles and described in various ways. However, using the generic purposes pursued by clients produces the following (Kuber, 1996):

*   *Achieving organisational purposes and objectives*, which covers sectoral leadership, competitive advantage, customer satisfaction, total quality management, total productivity, corporate excellence, high performance, improved business results, growth and similar concepts and terms reflecting the thinking and the priorities of both clients and consultants.

- *Solving management and business problems* to help managers and other decision makers with problem solving is a frequently mentioned purpose of consulting. The professional assistance involves identifying, diagnosing and solving problems concerning various areas and aspects of management and business.
- *Identifying and seizing new opportunities*, in which consulting firms are considered a source of valuable information and ideas that can be turned into a wide range of initiatives, innovations and improvements in any area of business. Examples include developing and motivating staff, optimising the use of financial resources, finding new business contacts and developing many ideas resulting in actions.
- *Enhancing learning* is one of the main contributors to the development of professional management consulting. Consulting assignments become learning assignments to empower the client by bringing new competence into the organisation and helping managers and staff to learn from their own and the consultant's experience.
- *Implementing changes* from the change agent (the new label given to the consultant), consultants help organisations understand change, live with change, and make changes needed for sustainable and successful operation.

As a management consultant, then, I am not only in a position to diagnose organisational problems, but must also suggest how enterprises should choose the social elements to be served in society. This is in order to effect the transformational modalities required to advance their organisation and make transitions, through their social systems, on the road to achieving a better quality of life and well-being. We now turn specifically to management consulting in Jordan.

Management Consulting in Jordan

Jordan is a small country with limited resources and with a total population of about five million people, according to the last census. The government's budget has always been in deficit. That is why Jordan depends on international and foreign aid.

A percentage of this aid is directed towards research and development projects, through providers of management consulting. There are many local consultancy providers, in addition to foreign consulting firms, that serve the public and/or private sectors. But there is a problem of an absence of government regulations to improve, or even control, the consulting business and assure professionalism in this vital discipline.

Jordan has started to implement a socio-economic transformation programme, which needs succinct consultation in many fields. This includes all the changes that should have happened as part of World Trade Organisation agreements, and other international agreements, such as the Free Trade Agreement with the United States of America and the European Jordanian Agreement with the European Commission.

The major types of consulting management that have emerged in Jordan during the last ten years are the following:

1. Privatisation consultation: Free markets and zones were created as part of the transition to privatisation. Jordan privatised major public factories such as the cement factory, as well as the communications, electricity and transportation sectors, plus many government service directorates. All of these consultation studies were given to

international firms because of donor fund conditions.

2. E-government is another form of transformation, aimed at transforming all governmental business into electronic services. This kind of transformation requires a great deal of consultation management, aimed at changing policies and procedures as well as entire processes and operations, along with building new capacities within organisations. Many tenders were issued related to the e-government project, by both local and foreign firms. TEAM Jordan received some contracts for capacity building for some government directorates. This will provide a basis for transformation towards e-government and for the socio-economic transformation of knowledge management.

3. TQM, which is of particular relevance here. Jordan's government has issued standards for the King Abdullah II Award for Excellence and Transparency: one for the public sector and another for the private sector. Many governmental organisations have been nominated for this award. TEAM's work plays a significant role because of its recent experience in this field, especially with international standards such as ISO 9000 and other national and international standards.

I now turn to a local Arab, cultural and spiritual context, to set alongside the more conventional, global and technocratic one.

An Arab and Islamic Indigenous Consulting Orientation

MUSTASHAR AND SHURA

In modern legal terminology, the word *Mustashar* (counsellor or advisor) has been adopted to mean a knowledgeable person whose counsel is sought in an important scientific, technical, political or juridical topic.

Shura (consultation) has several meanings, one of which is verbal negotiation and dialogue to reveal what is right. The aim is to arrive at what is correct after first becoming acquainted with and pondering over numerous points of view. In other words, *Shura* is submitting difficult problems in worldly and religious affairs to those who are known for their wide practical experience and wise counsel. It is listening to different opinions and deducing a suitable solution to the problem. *Shura* is taken from an old Arab saying: 'I have taken honey from its right place, or examined the mount and known how it walks' (Al-Tamimi, 2003).

Continued co-operation between the top management in the business world and the outside specialist yields good results, performance improvements and innovative methods. This is in addition to improved technical and behavioural skills, which, on the one hand, help with organisational progress and, on the other hand, independently build the science of management, with its special factors. However, the management consulting process is not a short-term one. It takes place over a period of time, when the client lacks technical expertise or is experiencing managerial problems. The consultant's effect on knowledge, culture and work skills, on employees and on the development process is an integral part of development.

We will now probe more deeply into *Shura* and, as we do so, it will become apparent that it is very different from the conventional, global wisdom on management consulting.

SIGNIFICANCE OF SHURA IN ISLAM

For Izzeddeen Al-Tamimi (2003), the significance of *Shura* is the following. It is an exigency of social life, a guarantee against the violation of rights, a form of worship, a focus for the development of faculties and an opportunity for affinity and amity. As such, it is significantly different in orientation from conventional management consultancy, much more social and cultural in effect, and relatively less technological and economic in orientation. Specifically:

- Shura is a necessity and *an exigency of social life*; no nation or community can do without it. It serves supreme national interests, and correct views are mostly generated through the interaction of different opinions and concepts.
- From an Islamic perspective, *Shura* entitles the nation to supervise its own affairs. It provides a basic *guarantee against violation of the state's constitution and abuses by those in power*. Guaranteeing egalitarianism, it embodies a great deal of co-operation between ruling authorities and the nation's deputies, who were chosen in general elections to represent the nation by providing opinions and discussions of social, political, economic and other aspects of life.
- In fact, practising *Shura* is a response to the call of Allah. It is *a form of worship* and obedience to Allah, which is a good enough reason for practising *Shura* in national and public life. Another aim of *Shura* is the search for and arrival at what is right. 'Wisdom is the quest for the faithful Muslim wherever he finds it.'
- Through *Shura, talents and capacities can be identified* and the mettle of men and women can be tested. *Shura* is a *field for the development of mental, behavioural and intellectual abilities* for those who practise it. Meanwhile, it is instrumental in co-ordination and mobilisation, and benefits from concerted efforts and their merits.
- *Shura* provides an *opportunity for affinity and amity* on the basis of faith, knowledge, beneficence and blessings. *Shura* is also a means for silencing harmful rumours and warding off lethal seditions.

For Pakistani-born, London-based contemporary Muslim scholar Ziauddin Sardar, 'Both *ijma* (consensus) and *shura* (consultation), are the basic and essential values of governance in any Muslim community. The process of consultation and consensual politics not only strengthens civic institutions within Muslim societies, but also legitimises pluralistic identities and interests within a Muslim community. Also *ijma* and *shura* ensure equality and justice by making consultation mandatory with all segments of society' (Sardar, 2006).

We now turn from consultancy in general, both the conventional Western and the Islamic Arab varieties, to the role consultants can play in transformation, a major theme of this book. Again, we start with a conventional, global–local perspective and then move on to the unconventional, local–global perspective adopted more specifically in this book.

How Consultants Can Help to Create Transformation: Conventional Perspective

Consultants can help to maintain business transformation in many different ways, providing a complete and exhaustive picture. Clients can choose from among many alternatives; however, most conventional, 'Westernised' consulting assistance to management will be given in one or more of the following ways, as mentioned by Kuber et al. in their guide to the profession (Kuber, 1996).

PROVIDING KNOWLEDGE AND INFORMATION

It can be knowledge: information on markets, customers, sectoral trends, raw materials, suppliers, competitors, potential partners, sources of engineering expertise, government policies and regulations or mandates. No consulting assignment is complete without working with knowledge and information that leads to providing better tactics and explicit knowledge. The society that possesses knowledge-power at the turn of this century can act locally and globally as a superpower. It can also initiate great transformations as a global social system.

PROVIDING SPECIALIST RESOURCES

A consultant can be used to supplement the client organisation's staff. Usually, these consultants will be specialists in areas where the client is looking for short-term expertise to improve many fields in the organisation in order to activate socio-organisational transformation as an institutionalised paradigm.

ESTABLISHING BUSINESS CONTACTS AND LINKAGES

Many clients turn to consultants in their search for new business contacts, agents, representatives, suppliers, subcontractors, joint ventures, merger partners, sources of funding and so on. The consultant's task may involve identifying one or more suitable experts to develop areas not sufficiently known to the client; these experts become hybrid gurus of transformation in their respective organisations.

PROVIDING EXPERT OPINION

The consultant may be approached to provide expert opinion in cases where the client can choose from among several alternatives and prefers to seek impartial and independent third-party advice before taking an important decision for the actualisation and realisation of the expected transformation.

DOING DIAGNOSTIC WORK

Diagnostic skills and instruments are among the consultant's principal assets. Therefore, clients use consultants for a wide range of diagnostic tasks regarding the organisation's strengths and weaknesses, positive and negative trends, potential for improvement, barriers to change and so on. This includes prescribing methods and new regimens for emerging innovation and the creativity needed for transformation.

DEVELOPING ACTION PROPOSALS

Effectively completed diagnostic work may be followed by the development of specific action proposals. This is in an area that was diagnosed as needing improvement and development for accomplishing socio-behavioural transformation in organisational and societal arenas. This triggers intra-organisational and inter-organisational transformation, congruent with social transition.

IMPROVING SYSTEMS AND METHODS

A major portion of all consulting services concern systems and methods in areas such as management information, business planning, operations scheduling and control, business process integration and management, inventory control, client-order processing, social benefits and other systems.

PLANNING AND MANAGING ORGANISATIONAL TRANSFORMATION

When the organisation has difficulties and feels insecure during the change process, the role of the consultant will be as a catalyst to create a suitable environment to deal with interpersonal relations, conflicts, lack of motivation, team building and other issues in the organisational and human behaviour field required for human emancipation.

LEARNING, AND DEVELOPING MANAGEMENT AND STAFF

While general-purpose learning is inherent in all consulting, the training and development of managers or staff can be a distinct client service provided in conjunction with support of other services. Alternatively, it can be provided as a separate service, considered as a stepping-stone for effective transformation.

PROVIDING PERSONAL COUNSELLING

Management consultants can render an excellent service to managers and entrepreneurs who need strictly personal feedback and relaxed, friendly advice on their leadership style, behaviour and work habits, relations with colleagues, weaknesses, and personal qualities that need to be better utilised.

It should now be obvious that management consulting can cover a wide range of areas for the development of business and top management in organisations, plus helping them with problem solving, progress and sustainability.

How Consultants Can Help to Create Transformation: Arab Perspective

PURSUING JUSTICE THROUGH MANAGEMENT CONSULTANCY IN CONTEXT

The question here is: Do we have a need for *Shura*-based consulting management in the Arab world to improve our society? Is it an incentive for the creation of transformation? The answer is: There is a great need. This is especially the case when considering the Arab Awakening that is taking place today. However, we are still in a transitional stage. Examples of this, lying between tradition (*al Shura*) and modernity (management consultancy), can be found in all developing countries.

Recently, we have seen that the number of management consultancy firms has increased dramatically, in Jordan specifically, if not also in the Arab world generally; but the general feeling is that these are neither integral, as per Arab spirit–Western technique, nor are they international, like a McKinsey or a PricewaterhouseCoopers. Also, on the one hand, the consulting profession in Jordan does not have any official, international regulations or laws by which to organise itself at this point in time. On the other hand, there is no specific management or consulting theory stemming from our roots and culture, such as I.Theory. So we are caught between two stools, one anonymous and inauthentic, the other parochial and patriarchal. How do we transcend this situation?

In effect, there is a need for management consulting that combines the local with the global: local culture with global technique. So our role as Arab management consultants is very important: to achieve transformation through our consultation process in the above local–global light. Islamic intellectuals like Sardar and Assaf are convinced that fertile ground for the application, and indeed evolution, of Islamic approaches lies in their ability to interact with all places and at all times, and through a framework that enables us to use different methods to achieve the ultimate value, which is justice, within each context.

What has this meant specifically, in the context of quality and transformation, for TEAM?

Conclusion

PHASE 1 – THINK GLOBALLY, ACT LOCALLY: TEAM'S ROLE IN QUALITY AND TRANSFORMATION

I will now trace my own consulting trajectory, from the global to the local, for TQM, and then from the local to the global, for I.Theory, set in the context of my role both as a management consultant and as a doctoral researcher and innovator in the Arab world.

Fifteen years ago, TEAM Jordan was a pioneer in offering services that the market needed as a result of globalisation. In 1995, I started an awareness campaign for global quality management systems standards such as ISO 9000, environmental management systems ISO 14000, in addition to hazard analysis and critical control points (HACCP) systems. These systems are global systems, now required everywhere. TEAM Jordan, as I have already intimated, has succeeded in qualifying more than 300 organisations to obtain international certification during the last ten years. We were thinking globally, acting locally.

This was a first, globally instigated step towards change management and transformation and, as such, I was acting as a conventional management consultant, based on a global definition of TQM, such as the following ISO definition (Abrahamson, 1996):

> *TQM is a management approach for an organisation, centred on quality, based on the participation of all members and aiming at long-term success through customer satisfaction, and benefits to all members of the organisation and to society.*

To obtain greater consistency of effort, such TQM required development in several respects. For example (Roys et al., 2006):

- Review and revise or design the strategy with vision, mission, and objectives, for all departments.
- Review and revise or design the organisational structure.
- Design and document all processes for all departments and draw all process maps.
- Review and revise or design all HR systems, such as: job description, recruitment, selection, orientation, performance, management training, needs assessment, succession system, HR planning and others.
- Develop and build knowledge management systems inside organisations.
- Create quality culture inside organisations through continual learning processes for all managerial and professional levels.
- Create a culture focusing on customers and deliver services or products with optimal quality levels that exceed their satisfaction and actually delight them.

This was basically the approach that I and my consultancy company, TEAM Jordan, adopted before, in the new millennium, I embarked upon my doctoral studies with TRANS4M, as a Centre for Social Innovation, with a view to thereby turning fundamental research into transformative action, local identity into global integrity.

PHASE 2 – TOWARD THE CENTRE – A (TRANS)CULTURAL TRANSFORMATION PROGRAMME

Ten years ago, as I have mentioned, starting in 2001, TEAM Jordan and the University of Buckingham (which partnered with TRANS4M), ran a master's programme in Transformation Management for senior managers in Jordan and the Middle East in public, private and civic organisations, with a particular transcultural orientation. In other words, the focus was on alternative approaches to management and transformation in the East and West, North and South, and the programme raised the question of what the role of the centre (the Middle East) was. Little did I realise at the time that I would be co-creating an answer: I.Theory.

My role in this unique programme, which operates locally and globally, and thereby transculturally, was to link organisations through a group of chief executives from all kinds of Jordanian public, private and civic enterprises, which were represented in the programme and aiming to transform their organisations conceptually and spiritually.

The overall focus was on cultural and social as well as economic and technological transformation and economic development; in other words, to take managers through a three-dimensional journey, as follows:

- Personal dreams and aspirations: developing a strong local/global desire to learn and build self-discipline.
- Organisational transformation: preparing their organisations for transformation by fusing tradition with modernity, accepting the challenge to meet the new (trans) cultural reality, keeping our cultural values at the core of such transformation.
- Societal transformation: realising that it is essential to involve the community and society in the transformational process, through a transcultural change process, drawing on the South, East, North and West, via our own centre.

In that context, management consulting becomes a necessary vehicle for helping individuals, organisations and societies to achieve their goals of sustainable development and transformation in an integral manner. The Islamic term *Shura* needs, then, to be seen in that integral light, whereby all worlds meet, through our centre.

PHASE 3 – CENTRING ON I.THEORY – FROM SHURA TO INTEGRAL CONSULTING

However, it was only once I had embarked on a TRANS4M-inspired doctoral programme, subsequent to the master's degree I completed in Jordan, that the light really began to dawn. Having been immersed for two years during my master's, and building on my prior lifetime of experience living and working in the Arab world, I finally began to realise that it was possible, and desirable, to link Arab/Islamic spirit with Western/global technique. Whereas in my youth, as a proud Palestinian-Jordanian, I was more political than spiritual in my orientation while pursuing a business and economic path, I now began to see a way whereby all of my life could be integrated.

I asked myself: How do I, then, specifically as a consultant, evolve the exogenous TQM philosophy, based on global standards, from West and East, through my own centre? This would need to include the building of a co-operative and communal, justice-laden Islamic environment with an enterprise, and creating a new organisational culture with Islamic values based on justice as a core value. Senior management, whether Islamic, Christian or indeed secular, would need to be committed to unifying individual and group objectives and moving corporations towards realising social as well as economic goals. The unification principle is the essence of I.Theory in a management context. This positions conflict and competition outside of the organisation and works to achieve the co-operative well-being of the organisation's members, who are the main players in the development process.

So, midway through the first decade of the new millennium, I was ready to adopt a local–global, indigenous–exogenous approach to both consultancy and management, bearing out the transformation of myself, my organisation and my society. Moreover, what I had internalised through my doctoral studies was that such a fundamental shift in orientation was underpinned by my underlying ontology (theory of reality), epistemology (theory of knowledge) and, ultimately, methodology (approach to knowledge creation). In order to become a transformative practitioner, linking myself as subject to the object of my activities, I needed to get to grips with this. With that in mind, we turn to Chapter 4.

PART II

Methodology

4 *Methodology: Towards an Integral Consultant*

Introduction

RE-VISIONING SCIENCE AND METHOD IN MANAGEMENT CONSULTING

I have already mentioned, in the previous chapter, that 'scientific management', so called, particularly that which prevailed in the first part of the twentieth century in America, was based on certain 'Western' premises. Atomism and individualism, objectivity and systematisation were all part of it, and it was in this allegedly 'scientific' climate that management consulting evolved. It was a distinct reflection, therefore, of a specifically Western worldview, in fact one that was increasingly challenged, in the West itself, in the latter part of the twentieth century, when subjective and intersubjective, as well as objective, knowledge has come increasingly to the fore. Positivism has been challenged by interpretivism and constructivism, whereby we co-evolve reality, rather than accepting it entirely as a given. Sad to say, conventional 'management consulting' has not evolved accordingly, although there are many individual consultants who operate according to this newly emerging, more integral paradigm.

That having been said, most of the re-visioning of knowledge creation has come from Europe or America, if not also from Japan. Seemingly nothing has come from the Arab region, where I am based. Whereas that region played a role during the ninth to thirteenth centuries in promoting a scientific renaissance, such has not been the case in modern times – with the exception of individual leaders of thought such as Ziauddin Sardar. However, the work in which I am engaged in reconstructing management and management consulting with a view to transforming individuals, organisations and societies locally–globally, so as to enable them to become more whole, builds on a particular approach to 'integral' and co-operative consultancy that is more inclusive than the more conventional 'scientific method'.

We now turn specifically to co-operative inquiry, and to the more integral approach (from both an epistemic and a political viewpoint) to consultancy that arises from it.

FROM SHURA TO CO-OPERATIVE INQUIRY IN CONSULTATION

I selected John Heron's *Co-operative Inquiry* as a means of co-evolving I.Theory, for two reasons. First, as we shall see, it is a methodology that is inclusive of many worlds, rather than being exclusive to one. Second, as a *co-operative* approach, it is coincident with the Islamic approach to *Shura*.

> *Heron established the Centre for Research into Human Potential at Surrey University in the seventies of the twentieth century, and has spent the past thirty years researching and developing methods of co-operative inquiry, both informative and trans-formative. The self generating culture he has sought to promote, then, is a community whose members are continuously adopted, periodically reviewed and altered in the light of experience, reflection and ever deepening vision. Its participants continually recreate it through cycles of collaborative inquiry in living and working together. (Lessem, 2004)*

In the first place, co-operative inquiry, epistemically, so to speak, incorporates four knowledge modes: experiential, imaginal, conceptual and practical. In fact these modes are altogether integral in that, in the terms used by TRANS4M, they are Southern (experiential), Eastern (imaginal), Northern (conceptual) and Western (practical) in orientation. Second, and politically, so to speak, co-operative inquiry is inherently participative and democratic, research and innovation being undertaken 'with' rather than 'on' people.

Co-operative inquiry involves two or more people researching and developing a topic or problem through their experience with it, using a series of cycles in which they move between experience and reflection. The methodology is distinct both in its co-operative approach and in its encompassing four ways of knowing, as follows:

1. Experiential
2. Imaginal
3. Conceptual
4. Practical (Heron, 1996).

Moreover, the link between *Shura*, as consultation, and the co-operative inquiry approach is strong. It is the norm for Muslims to consult before making decisions. The principles of *Shura* are similar to the notion of democracy; and co-operative inquiry depends on democracy among co-operative researchers.

For Sardar (2006), '*Ijma* and *Shura* are the basic and essential values of governance in any Muslim community. The process of consultation and consensual politics not only strengthens civic institutions within Muslim societies but also legitimises pluralistic identities and interests within Muslim community.' He adds: 'The participatory structures of governance based on *Ijma* and *Shura* ensure equality and justice by making consultation mandatory with all segments of society.'

In fact, as a researcher and consultant, and altogether as a social innovator, I have also drawn on the case-study method of Robert Yin (2003) to co-evolve I.Theory with co-operative inquirers at RSCN (public, civic and environmental sectors) and at Al-Quds Paints Co. (private sector). The two methods complement one another. The first wing of Heron's methodology is epistemic knowledge, and the preparation of Yin's case studies involves gathering information. In epistemic knowledge, field procedures are performed co-operatively and data is collected from existing people. Participation is thus the common denominator between Heron and Yin. I now turn more specifically to co-operative inquiry.

Co-operative Inquiry and Integral Consultancy

EPISTEMIC AND POLITICAL

Co-operative inquiry, and thereby integral consultancy, has two wings:

- Epistemic (knowledge based on and formed by truth values): This is subjective, because it is known only through the form that the mind gives to it; and objective, because the mind interpenetrates the given cosmos that it shapes. This also asserts the participative relationship between the knower and the known, the consultant and the consulted.
- Political (values based): This relates to social participation, in which there is a mutually enabling balance, in addition to the participative features of decision making. This involves:
  - participation through empathetic communion and imagining, whereby knowing is mutual awakening, again between consultant and consulted
  - participation in both explicit and tacit knowledge sharing, and creating processes
  - uniting the knower (subject) with the known (object)
  - the integration of the three stages which reflect the human being's, as well as the organisation's (if not the whole of society's) stages of development – from childhood to ego development, then to mature integration.

This thus gives a whole new tone to 'integral' consultancy, both knowledge-wise and participation-wise.

CONSULTING AS PARTICIPATION

Co-operative inquiry, emerging as integral consultancy, is a form of participation that consults with rather than about people. In fact, from the start of my work on this book, I have been engaged with my colleague Dr Assaf, a senior TEAM consultant who created I.Theory (Assaf, 2005), in co-operation whereby, between the two of us:

- Decisions about content and method arose in a process of shared consultation.
- There was, between Assaf and me, an intentional interplay between reflection and making sense, on the one hand, and experience and action, on the other.
- Explicit attention was given, to some extent at least, to the validity of our inquiries, especially with a view to how things would work out on the ground.
- I.Theory is both informative and transformative in its orientation.

Ken Wilber (1983), the renowned contemporary American social philosopher, similarly to both Heron and TRANS4M, has proposed that we need to focus on four areas of concern, which he terms four quadrants:

- cultural inter-subjectivity (we) connected with the *experiential*
- social structure and function (it) connected with the *conceptual*
- individual subjectivity (i) closely connected with the *imaginal*
- personal behaviour (our) connected with the *practical*.

Co-operative inquiry, and thereby integral consultancy, integrates all the above, and for Heron, as indeed for my colleagues Ronnie Lessem and Alexander Schieffer at TRANS4M, adds a fifth dimension:

- the reality of integral lived experience that arises through empathetic communion.

What does this imply for our co-operative, integral approach to research and consultancy? There are four elements to such participation as an integral consultant:

1. Propositions about human experience that are the outcome of consultation are of questionable validity if they are not grounded in the consultant's, or indeed the consulted's, experience.
2. The most rigorous way to do this is for consultants to ground the statements they come up with directly in their experience as co-subjects with the consulted, where this experience involves a deep kind of participative (as opposed to merely objective) knowing.
3. As the human condition is one of shared and dialogic embodiment, the consultant can operate only through the full range of his or her sensibilities, rather than exclusively as an analyst, in a relationship of reciprocal dialogue.
4. This enables consultants, as well as those consulted, to come to know not only the external forms – conceptual and practical, individual and collective – but also their inner aspects – experiential and imaginal.

With the Islamic values and management practices on quality and transformation (inner aspects), with the long experience I have of QM and TQM (outer forms), and with my involvement in the transformation management programme (which aims to integrate the inner with the outer) – also involving customers in a participative process of knowing – the epistemological basis is secured. In addition, through the implementation of I.Theory and its HR systems components, we follow Heron's sequential steps for epistemic participation with customers.

Finally, and in summary, the reasons for 'political' participation in the consulting process are:

- The consulted have a right to participate in the consulting process. The purpose is to formulate knowledge about and through them.
- This gives them the opportunity to identify and express their own preferences and values.
- It empowers those consulted to flourish as full persons in an informative or transformative consulting enterprise – indeed, as co-creators in it.
- It avoids their being disempowered, oppressed and misrepresented, in any unilateral consulting design, by implicit values of the consultant's.

We now turn specifically to consulting as knowledge creation.

Integral Consulting as Epistemically Based Co-operative Inquiry

THE FOUR KNOWLEDGE MODES

Systemic logic, as deployed in co-operative inquiry (Heron) and in integral consulting (TEAM Jordan) holds that:

- Experiential (empathetic) knowledge is evident in meeting and feeling the presence of some energy, entity, person, place, process or thing.
- Presentational or imaginal knowledge is evident in the intuitive grasp of the significance of patterns expressed in graphic, musical, plastic or verbal art forms.
- Conceptual or propositional knowledge is ultimately interdependent with the three other kinds of knowledge.
- Practical knowledge is evident in exercising skill.

Whereas conceptual, if not also practical, knowledge comes as second nature to the conventional consultant, experiential and imaginal knowledge lie beyond their ken. In fact, it is this very lack of an ability to imagine and to empathise that prevents the average, 'Westernised' consultant from immersing themselves in another world.

THE 'UP-HIERARCHY'

Moreover, for the integral consultant:

1. Experiential knowing lies at the base of a 'knowledge pyramid', comprising the direct, live 'being-in-the-world'. For us, such 'experiential' knowing in our consulting business underlies quality and transformation, as viewed through the co-operative methodology, and it provides the basis for all managerial theories, specifically through I. Theory with all its norms.
2. Imaginal or presentational knowing depends on people working with each other, as consultant and consulted, so that imaginal knowing, in this context, is based on culture, if not also on nature, whereby the nature of human thought and a relationship is a creative one.
3. Propositional or conceptual knowledge: after studying and analysing all kinds of exogenous managerial theories related to quality and transformation, which includes Western theories based on freedom values, or the Japanese theory based on social equality, I shall draw upon I.Theory, including its prospective implementation.
4. Practical knowing, the exercise of skill: the aim of ultimate practice is to ensure the application of the knowledge acquired; therefore, we must put our knowledge into a practical context. Moreover, practical knowing, or know-how, is the consummation of the knowledge quest. It is grounded in and empowered by the prior forms of knowing, and immediately supported by the propositional knowing of I.Theory, which it celebrates and affirms at a higher level. It affirms what is intrinsically worthwhile by manifesting itself in action.

This dynamic 'up-hierarchy' is different from the classic top-down one, which controls everything from above, without being empowered by any of it. It also follows that practical knowledge (knowing how to exercise the skill), supported by conceptual knowledge, is underpinned by imaginal and experiential knowledge, all together providing the integral basis for I.Theory. The pyramid, in effect, can be seen as a spiral that expands our knowing and is free and unfettered – or constricts if we are socially damaged.

I now turn to the basis of the relationship between co-operative inquiry, integral consultancy and the case study approach of Robert Yin, which I will also be adopting in order to practise the skills that are connected with transformative action based on co-operative and participative values.

The Case Study Approach

ISSUES TO BE ADDRESSED

The two case applications, RSCN and Al Quds Paint Co., were deliberately selected to cover contextual conditions in the Arab world and to address the main issues at hand:

- What is the effect of Islamic theory on achieving quality?
- What role does management by values/the I.Theory in Jordan play in charting a developmental transformation bearing upon quality?
- How does integral consultancy work out in practice?

CASE STUDY METHOD

Any case-study inquiry does the following:

- Copes with the technically distinctive situation in which there will be many variables of interest.
- Relies on multiple sources of evidence.
- Benefits from the prior development of theoretical propositions to guide data collection and analysis.

Based on the first wing of Heron's co-operative inquiry, epistemic knowledge, the preparation for each case study should cover background information about the project, the substantive issues being investigated and relevant readings about the issues. The basis of epistemic knowledge is to undertake the research phase of the integral consultancy, with a view to subsequent transformation, co-operatively and to collect experiential as well as factual data from existing people and situations. In this sense, the research or informative phase of integral consulting, as per co-operative inquiry, involves reciprocal dialogue, as well as data gathering, and reflects the experiential and imaginal, as well as the conceptual and practical aspects of knowledge creation.

Moreover, at the heart of the case-study method is a set of substantive questions reflecting the actual inquiry, including some generated by the subjects of the inquiry themselves. Here, it is necessary to interact with explicit and tacit knowledge so as to be able to arrive at all four modes of knowledge.

To ensure distinct and subjective participation, five types of question related to Yin's methods need to be used:

1. Questions asked of, and generated by, specific interviewees.
2. Questioned arising out of an individual case as a whole.
3. Questions asked across multiple cases, for example RSCN and Al Quds Paints Co.
4. Questions asked of an entire study – calling on information beyond the cases, including the literature drawn upon.
5. Normative questions about policy recommendations and conclusions that go beyond the narrow scope of the study.

Most commonly, for Yin's method, case-study interviews are of an open-ended nature, in which we ask key respondents about the facts of a matter, as well as for opinions about events, together with, in some cases, their insight into events. We then use these responses as a basis for further inquiry in which evoking of questions and insights from the interviewees, both individually and collectively, group interviews, and knowledge sharing and, indeed, creation are actively encouraged.

In Heron's co-operative approach, these types of interview serve to reinforce the political participation: to formulate knowledge about and through people based on social participation, and to assure the right of participation in the consultation process. This gives interviewees the opportunity to identify their own preferences and values, and also empowers them to flourish as full persons in the informative, and subsequently transformative, co-creative exercise. In my own case, such co-creation will lead to the further evolution of I.Theory.

Conclusion

I began this chapter by indicating that the kind of transformation with which I have been engaged – ultimately through the development and application of I.Theory as a local–global, indigenous–exogenous approach to quality and transformation – required a whole new approach to that undertaken by conventional management consultants. Such an approach needed to be subjective as well as objective, experiential and imaginative, as well as conceptual and practical, and one (*Shura*-wise) that worked *with* those participating, rather than doing something to them.

The closest equivalent to this in the 'research' and methodological repertoire, is co-operative inquiry (CI), albeit in my case also reinforced by the case-study method. CI has three *integral* attributes that lend themselves to an ultimately 'integral' approach to consultancy. Firstly, it combines the informative (research) with the transformative (innovation), and as such can be easily aligned with consultancy, as well as with pure research. Secondly, it is both epistemically (knowledge-wise) rich, thereby encompassing several diverse worlds, and also politically (participation-wise) inclusive, in that informative and transformative phases are undertaken with, rather than on, those consulted. Thirdly, it combines action and reflection, in a continual alternation between the two.

From a Middle Eastern perspective, whereby, when our culture and society has been at its best it has served to balance and integrate the North (Europe) and the South (Africa), the East (Asia) and the West (globalisation), CI is a good source of such differentiation and integration. To the extent, as we shall see, that I.Theory (justice) is both distinct from, but also inclusive of, Japanese (equality) and American (freedom) approaches, co-operative inquiry, with its rich epistemic mix, is a good methodological foundation on which to build.

Now I will turn from methodology to content, generally and specifically. Generally, I will:

- introduce the Japanese and American concepts of TQM (Chapter 5)
- focus on quality in Islam (Chapter 6).

Specifically, I will then:

- compare I.Theory with other, more conventional management models (Chapter 7)
- probe further into the managerial philosophies underlying these major models (Chapter 8)
- explore Islamic values (Chapter 9)
- and present applied systems that incorporate my further evolution of I.Theory (Chapter 10).

Thereafter we shall move from context, methodology and content to application, through the two case studies, and finally to the conclusions.

PART III

Content

CHAPTER 5

Total Quality and Transformation

Introduction

FROM CONTEXT AND METHODOLOGY TO CONTENT

I have now set the context, that is, the story of my life and work, the consultancy I established and Jordan, the country in which I have spent most of my life. I have also described a methodology, I.Theory, that has enabled me to evolve, as an integral consultant, an I.Consultant so to speak.

This part of the book covers six chapters (5 to 10). They cover, firstly and generally, the origins of quality, quality in Islam and its historical development, and a comparison with the two global theories in TQM: the Japanese theory and the Western (US). Secondly and specifically, I will attempt to identify the gaps in these theories and how I.Theory fills them, especially in view of all the critiques of ISO standards and TQM systems. Finally, I will explain all the values related to I.Theory, with a focus on justice as a core value and the application systems that I have evolved.

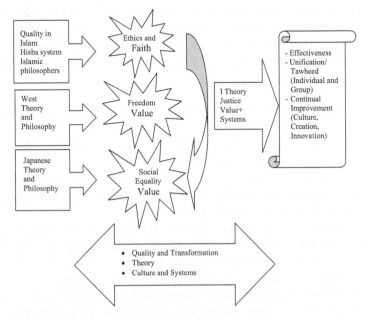

Figure 5.1   Classification of content (Chapters 5–10)

In this chapter I cover some historical issues related to the concept of quality, starting with *Itqan* in Arabic, which means quality. In fact, 1,400 years ago Prophet Mohammad focused on *Itqan* as a lifestyle and linked it with God's love. We now turn to quality in general.

ORIENTATION TO QUALITY

Quality here is based on ethics and good performance, irrespective of what the performance standards are. It is related to the faith and beliefs of humankind, and not just to measurements and inspections. In that respect it forms a good bridge between philosophy and technique, and a good starting-point for integral consulting. There are many indicators for quality in work in the nineteenth and early twentieth centuries. For instance, Frederick Taylor, as we have seen, focused on scientific management in order to achieve quality. He focused on management functions, and separated planning functions from execution functions. In this context, management has two styles. One is concerned with functions and processes and the other relies, in addition to functions and processes, on the ideology or philosophy prevalent in the organisational culture or value system.

After the Second World War, two American consultants, Deming and Juran, introduced statistical quality control techniques to the Japanese to help them in their rebuilding efforts. Therefore, in this chapter I focus on the Western and Japanese thinkers, starting with Deming, who was the bridge between the US and Japan. He introduced the 14 principles of quality and the chain reaction to improve quality. I follow this with Juran, who introduced the Trilogy (Quality Planning, Control, and Improvement) and the 10 steps to achieving quality.

This chapter also covers the two notable Japanese figures in the quality domain: Ishikawa and Taguchi. Ishikawa was the famous figure in Japanese quality who focused on the development of the participatory problem-solving method. Taguchi focused on testing products, and measuring variations from the target value of specification.

The implementation of TQM in Japan through its thinks and their ideology was one of the factors behind that country's success. The Americans raised the question: If Japan is able to achieve excellence, why not us? I shall answer that question in Chapter 6.

The History and Importance of Quality in America and Japan

Quality is not a new concept in modern business. Prophet Mohammad said more than 1,400 years ago: 'Allah loves to see one's job done at the level of Itqan' (Saheeh Muslim, vol. 17). Here, quality means the following: less cost, good quality, right time and right quantity. Prophet Mohammad used the word *Itqan* in Arabic, which means perfection or best practice. I cover this in the next chapter.

In October 1887, William Cooper Procter, grandson of the founder of Procter & Gamble, told his employees: 'The first job we have is to turn out quality merchandise that consumers will buy, and keep on buying. If we produce it efficiently and economically, we will earn a profit, in which you share' (Evans and Lindsay, 2001).

Procter's statement addresses three issues that are critical to the managers of manufacturing and service organisations: productivity, cost and quality. Productivity (the measure of efficiency defined as the amount of output achieved per unit of input), cost of operations, quality of goods and services that create profitability. The most significant factor in determining the success or failure of any organisation in the long run is quality. Optimal quality of goods or services can provide an organisation with competitive edge. Utmost quality reduces costs, due to fewer returns, less reworking and less scrap. Quality increases productivity, profits and other measures of success. Most importantly, good quality generates satisfied, loyal customers who reward the organisation with continued patronage and favourable word-of-mouth advertising.

During the Middle Ages in Europe, a skilled craftsperson was both manufacturer and inspector. Quality assurance was informal; every effort was made to ensure that quality was built into the final product by the people producing it. From the middle of the eighteenth century until the twentieth century there were many examples of quality, such as the French gunsmith Honor Le Blanc, who developed a system for manufacturing muskets to a standard pattern, using interchangeable parts.

In the early 1900s, the work of Fredrick W. Taylor (Society of Automotive Engineers, 1981), often called the Father of Scientific Management, led to a new philosophy of production. Taylor's philosophy was to separate the planning function from the execution function. Managers and engineers were given the task of planning, supervisors and workers the task of execution. This approach worked well, and the quality was there. This approach is management by laws, and eventually production organisations created separate quality departments.

Henry Ford, one of the leaders of the mass-production revolution, developed many of fundamentals of what we call 'total quality practices' in the early 1900s. This was discovered when Ford executives visited Japan in 1982 to study Japanese management practices and found that the bible of Japanese managers was Ford's book *My Life and Work*, written in 1926.

The early pioneers of quality assurance, Walter Shewhart, George Edward and others, including Edward Deming, developed many useful techniques for improving quality and solving quality problems. During the Second World War, the US military began using statistical sampling procedures and imposing stringent standards on its suppliers. After the war, during the late 1940s and early 1950s, a shortage of civilian consumer goods in the United States made production a top priority. In most companies, quality was not a priority for top managers, who delegated this responsibility to quality managers. During this time, two US consultants, Dr Joseph Juran and Dr W. Edwards Deming, introduced statistical quality control techniques to aid the Japanese in their rebuilding efforts. They focused on upper management rather than on quality specialists alone. With the support of top managers, the Japanese integrated quality throughout their organisations and developed a culture of continued improvement (*Kai-Zen*).

Improvement in Japanese quality was slow and steady; some 20 years passed before the quality of Japanese products exceeded that of Western manufacturers. By the 1970s, primarily due to the higher quality levels of their products, Japanese companies had penetrated significantly into Western markets.

The decade of the 1980s was a period of remarkable change and growing awareness of quality on the part of customers, industry and government in the United States, especially when they noticed differences in quality between Japanese- and US-made products, and people began to expect and demand high quality and reliability in goods and services, at a fair price.

The quality revolution in the US started in 1980, when Deming made a television programme entitled *If Japan Can … Why Can't We?* (Evans, 2001). Deming was the bridge between Japan and the US. He had helped to transform Japanese industry three decades earlier, and he also helped US companies from 1980 until his death in 1993. We now turn our attention to quality and transformation, with more of focus on the 'soft' cultural principles underlying it.

Quality and Culture Underlying Transformation

Any organisational activity can be viewed from one of three perspectives, depending on the intensity of the commitment to the activity:

- Function: a task or group of tasks to be performed that contribute to the mission and purpose of an organisation.
- Process: a set of steps, procedures or policies that define how a function is to be performed and what results are expected.
- Ideology: a set of values or beliefs that guide an organisation in the establishment of its vision, mission, strategy, objectives, processes and functions.

Many managers view quality as a set of tasks to be performed by specialists in quality control. Other managers have broader perspectives and see quality as a process and sub-processes in which many people at the operating level (from a number of functional areas of the organisation) are involved in cross-functional activities. Still other managers take the broadest view, in which quality is an ideology or philosophy that pervades and defines the culture of the entire organisation; for total quality (TQ) to truly succeed, it must define the culture of the organisation. Other managers view quality as holistic functions, practices and activities that must be implemented in all organisations.

A corporate culture is a company's value system and collection of guiding principles. The mission and vision statements of organisations often demonstrate cultural values. Culture is a powerful influence on behaviour, as mentioned above, and is reflected in a company's management, policies and actions. Thus, organisations that believe in the principles of TQ are more likely to implement those practices successfully. Likewise, actions set a culture in motion. Behaviour leads people to think in a certain way. Thus, as TQ practices are used routinely within an organisation, so its people learn to believe in the principles, and cultural changes can occur.

A concise summary of the principles on which learning, high-performing TQ organisations are built and managed is given in the following set of 'Core Values and Concepts' that form the basis of the Baldrige Criteria:

- Visionary leadership
- Customer-driven excellence
- Organisational and personal learning
- Valuing employees and partners
- Agility
- Focus on the future
- Management for innovation

- Management by fact
- Public responsibility and citizenship
- Focus on results and creating value
- Systems perspective.

These values must become a living, breathing part of the organisation's culture. Often they are embodied in the strategies and leadership philosophies of major organisations. For example, the TQ philosophy at Procter & Gamble focuses on superior consumer satisfaction. It is a statement of purpose that captures the 'what' and 'how' expected of their quality efforts. A similar philosophy is used in the American Express quality leadership approach. The fundamental beliefs about quality that provide the philosophical underpinning and guide decision making at American Express are:

- Quality is the foundation of continued success.
- Quality is a journey of continued improvement and innovation.
- Quality provides a high return, but requires the investment of time and resources.
- Quality requires committed leadership.
- Quality begins by meeting or exceeding the expectations of the customers and employees and stakeholders.
- Quality requires teamwork and learning at all levels.
- Quality comes from the energy of a community of motivated and skilled people who are given authority and take responsibility.

To understand and implement these concepts as a TQ philosophy, I require organisations to create cultural change/transformation.

Most traditional practices stem from fundamental structures of US business that are derived from Adam Smith's principles based on individual freedom and Fredrick Taylor's era of scientific management (Taylorism). Even though they were quite appropriate in their time and contributed to past economic success, these principles no longer suffice. Japan, in contrast, built its management system on the teachings of Deming, Juran, Peter Drucker and other modern business philosophers, whose focus relied on fundamental TQ principles.

We now turn specifically to TQM, which, over the past 50 years, has become a field in itself.

Total Quality Management

ORIENTATION TO TQM

In general, TQM is a process for managing quality, a philosophy for perpetual improvement in everything we do. It is also a set of guiding principles that represent the foundation of an organisation that is continuously improving towards transformation. TQM implies the mobilisation of the whole organisation to satisfy customer demand by focusing on the involvement and participation of everyone in the organisation for the systematic improvement of quality.

TQM provides a habit of improvement and development in all activities and at all levels by creating a positive environment and applying quantitative methods, analytical technique, expanding knowledge and growing expertise in process improvement. For D. Goetsch and S. Davis (Goetsch and Davis, 1995, 2002), 'Total Quality is not just one individual concept. It is a number of related concepts pulled together to create a comprehensive approach to doing business. Many people contributed in meaningful ways to the development of the various concepts that are known collectively as total quality.'

THE SPECIFIC ELEMENTS OF TQM

S.N. Chary (Chary, 2007) has explained the specific TQM elements as being the following.

1. Total customer satisfaction

The traditional view of quality has been 'corrective' (quality control) or at best 'preventive' (quality planning). Corrective actions ensure that defective products do not slip through and get into the consignment that is to be shipped to the customer. Preventive action ensures that the occasions to take corrective action are few and far between.

TQM looks at quality as a value provided to the customer. It is a methodology for maximising value to the organisation's customers, in order to ensure total satisfaction for customers.

2. Totality of functions

Every function in any job to be done, such as marketing, logistics, production or operation, purchasing, engineering or product design, has to be actively and fully involved. All functions are interrelated and interdependent, as in a symphony.

3. Total range of products and/or services

TQM should not be stopped after being applied to a select few of the company's products and services, because the customer cannot be offered some products that are good and others that are not so good. One product or service has an effect on the other, and the images of the products overlap in the customer's mind.

4. Addressing all aspects and dimensions of quality

The excellence of all dimensions of quality, such as responsiveness, courtesy, communication, competence, reliability, credibility and security, are determinants of TQM.

5. Quality instilled into everything

All of these products, services, processes, people, resources and interactions should be of a quality and suitable to the customer's needs and expectations. TQM has to address all these factors.

6. Satisfying both the internal and the external customers

In the context of supply chains, it is clear that the company will not be able to satisfy the ultimate customer unless it satisfies the immediate customer in the supply chain (internal customer).

7. Retain present customers, improve profits and generate new business

TQM is a means to an organisation's competitive survival, as well as to maintain and develop its healthy existence so that it can keep contributing to the economy and society. To achieve that end, it needs to retain current customers and generate new, adequate returns on investment, in addition to increasing the number of customers or generating new business. TQM has to facilitate organisational rejuvenation.

8. Total involvement in the organisation

Another element in improving processes and systems concerns the people who develop, deliver or handle these processes or systems, and entails the following:

- Develop employees' technical and/or interaction skills relevant to their jobs.
- Keep employees informed about related aspects such as: specific customer needs, specific market development, organisation's mission and vision, organisation's policies and procedures, values, regulations and so on.
- Widen employees' knowledge about the organisational culture and philosophy.

9. Leadership and commitment

The leadership of an organisation should develop the desired culture and instill it as a requirement for transformation. Also, the senior management should show the way to developing value systems, attitudes and behaviours so as to get all the levels of employees involved in the organisation's activities and programmes. It is the commitment of senior management that drives the process of transformation within the organisation.

CRITICISM OF TQM

At first glance, these elements sound reasonable; but further examination reveals that there is a need for greater attention to the interests of individuals (employees) and those of the group (management) inside the organisation in order to create the willingness to apply the above-mentioned critique and exceed customers' expectations.

TQM is rather vague or imprecise in defining what needs to be achieved. Total customer satisfaction is fine, but does a TQM programme translate that into exact requirements? In this respect, TQM is accused of ignoring detailed requirements.

TQM is general in nature. It is about the goal of any programme of quality improvement. So any such programme, including TQM, attempts to reach the quality level expected by the customer. According to its critics, the customers may not know what more to expect. We will now look at the overall philosophies underlying TQM.

TOTAL QUALITY PHILOSOPHIES

Deming's philosophy and contributions

Dr W. Edwards Deming has had a great influence on quality management. He gained a PhD in physics and was trained as a statistician. Much of his philosophy is based in these roots. From 1920 to 1930, he worked in statistical quality control for Western Electric. Deming recognised the importance of running the management process statistically. During the Second World War he taught quality control to engineers and factory workers as part of the US national defence effort.

After the war, he was invited to Japan to help the country rebuild; consequently, he began to teach statistical quality control in that country. His thinking went beyond mere statistics, however, and he focused on top-management leadership, customer/supplier partnerships and continuous improvement in product development and manufacturing processes. Japanese managers embraced these ideas, and Deming's influence on Japanese industry was so great that the Union of Japanese Scientists and Engineers established the Deming Application Prize in 1951 to recognise companies that show a high level of achievement in quality practices.

Deming lived in Washington, and his goal was to change entire perspectives in management. His philosophy focuses on making improvements in product or service quality by reducing uncertainty and variability in the design and manufacturing process. The Deming 'chain reaction' theory summarises his view (Figure 5.2). The improvements in quality lead to lower costs, due to less reworking, fewer mistakes, fewer delays and snags and better use of time and materials. Lower cost, in turn, leads to productivity improvements. With better quality and lower prices, a firm can achieve a higher market share and thus stay in business, providing more and more jobs. Deming stressed that top management has the overriding responsibility for quality improvements.

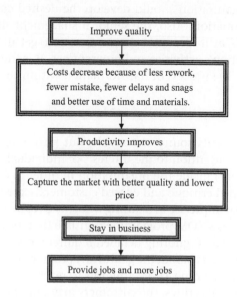

Figure 5.2   The Deming chain reaction

Source: Evans and Lindsay (2001), p. 91

Deming's philosophy as preached in 1985 included the following 14 points to help people transform their businesses (Deming, 1986):

- Create and publish to all employees a statement of the aims and purposes of the company or other organisation. The management must demonstrate constantly its commitment to this statement. Deming suggested that the company's principal role was to stay in business in order to provide jobs. It accomplishes this through innovation, research, constant improvement and self-maintenance.
- Adopt the new philosophy for top management and everybody. What Deming proposed was a new philosophy. We are in a new economic age, created in Japan, driven by computer speed and accuracy. We can no longer live with previously accepted levels of delays, mistakes, defective materials and defective workmanship. The pathway for change is a 'learning organisation' in which constant defects, uncorrected errors and negativism are unacceptable.
- Understand the purpose of inspection for improvement of processes and reduction of cost; which means eliminating the need for mass inspection to achieve quality by building quality into the product in the first place. In this case, the organisation can divert its attention to monitoring consumer satisfaction.
- End the practice of awarding business solely on the basis of price, and instead require quality along with price. The aim of reducing total cost by moving towards a single supplier for any one item and by developing long-term relationships of loyalty and trust is to constantly and always improve the system of production and service.
- Institute training to improve constantly and for ever every process for planning, production and service. Search continually for problems, in order to improve every activity in the company, to improve quality and productivity, and thus to constantly decrease costs. Institute innovation and constant improvement of product, service and process.
- Teach and institute leadership to keep up with changes in materials, methods, product and service design, machinery, techniques and services. Too often, workers have learned their job from other workers who were never trained. Employ good training and retrain often.
- Drive out fear, create trust and create a climate for innovation through adopting and instituting leadership aimed at helping people do their best. Improvement of quality will automatically improve productivity if immediate action is taken on reports of inherent defects, maintenance requirements, poor tools, fuzzy operational definitions and all conditions detrimental to quality.
- Optimise the achievement of the company's aims and purposes through the faster enhancement of the efforts of teams, groups and staff by eliminating fear throughout the organisation. It is necessary that people feel secure and ask questions.
- Eliminate exhortations to the workforce by breaking down barriers between departments and staff areas. Units that do not work as teams cannot force or address common workplace or industry-wide problems. Problem solving in isolation creates problems for others. People from different areas must join in teams to solve problems from a multidisciplinary perspective.
- (a) Eliminate numerical quotas for production. Instead, learn and institute methods for improvement. (b) Eliminate management by objectives (MBO). Instead, learn the capabilities of processes and how to improve them.

- Remove barriers that rob people of pride in workmanship. Substitute training aids and helpful leadership in order to achieve continual improvement.
- Encourage education and self-improvement for everyone. This implies, among other things, abolition of merit rating and of MBO. People are eager to do a good job and become distressed when they cannot. Too often, misdirection, faulty equipment and defective materials stand in the way of good performance.
- Take action to accomplish the transformation, because an organisation needs not just good people; it needs people who are improving with education. Advances in competitive position will have their roots in advancing knowledge in the field of endeavour.
- Commit everyone. A critical mass of people in the company must understand the 14 points. Support is not enough: constant and persistent action is required. The transformation is everybody's job.

Deming's 14 points constitute the core of his suggestions for achieving excellence, and cannot be implemented selectively; they are an all-or-nothing commitment. The 14 points summarise Deming's views on what a company must do in order to effect a positive transition from business as usual to world-class quality. He also identified the Seven Deadly Diseases to be eliminated or whose impact on TQ should be reduced:

1. Lack of consistency of purpose in planning products and services.
2. Emphasis on short-term profits.
3. Personal review systems for managers, and MBO without providing methods or resources.
4. Job hopping by managers.
5. Using only visible data and information in decision making.
6. Excessive medical costs.
7. Excessive costs of liability, driven up by lawyers.

In addition to the 14 points and the Seven Deadly Diseases, Deming's contributions to quality include the Deming Cycle.

The Deming Cycle

The Deming Cycle, illustrated in Figure 5.3, reflects the link between production and consumer needs and focuses the resources of all departments on a co-operative effort to meet those needs. The Deming Cycle proceeds as follows:

- Conduct the consumer research and use it in planning the product (Plan).
- Produce the product (Do).
- Check the product to make sure it was produced in accordance with the plan (Check).
- Market the product (Act).
- Analyse how the product is received in the marketplace in terms of quality, cost and other criteria (Analyse).

Figure 5.3 is very well known and most consultants use it in many management areas, such as strategic planning.

Plan your work; Do it (of course with quality); Check the results; take corrective actions or preventive actions with Act; and then Analyse the results. So, the Deming Cycle is PDCAA; however, many consultants omit the Analysis stage and end up with PDCA only.

The implementation of the Deming Cycle is an important step towards quality management.

In her book *The Deming Management Method* (Walton, 1986), an interpretation of Deming's 14 points along with the Seven Deadly Diseases that endanger a company's vitality, Mary Walton focuses on the Deming complete overhaul of an organisation's infrastructures rather than attempting a patchwork of sorts, and the distinction between a stable system and an unstable one. It follows from this that the responsibility for ensuring stability falls to management. Walton elaborates on these points and presents an extended analysis.

Walton looks at Deming's 'chain reaction' theory and notes that, through the improvement of quality, an organisation's costs go down and fewer mishaps occur. In addition, the continual reduction of mistakes, along with continually improving quality, translates into lower and lower costs. More important still is how the product or service is marketed. Even if a company has a product of value, it first has to place it on the market, and package it as an attractive commodity. Applied behaviour analysis offers a case in point regarding this.

We now turn from Deming to his fellow American, Juran.

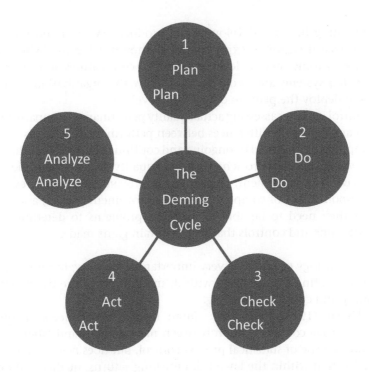

Figure 5.3   The Deming Cycle

Juran's philosophy and contributions

Joseph M. Juran was born in Romania in 1904 and came to the USA in 1912. He held degrees in both engineering and law. The Emperor of Japan awarded him the Order of the Sacred Treasure medal in recognition of his efforts to develop quality in Japan. He joined Western Electric in 1920 as it was pioneering the development of statistical methods for quality. His *Quality Control Handbook* is considered one of the most comprehensive quality manuals ever written.

Like Deming, Juran taught quality principles to the Japanese in 1950s and he was a principal force in their quality reorganisation. He agreed with Deming's critique of the US business crisis on account of the huge costs of poor quality and the loss of sales to foreign competition. Juran proposed a simple definition of quality: 'fitness for use'. This definition suggests that quality be viewed from both external and internal perspectives that relate to:

1. Customer satisfaction.
2. Freedom from product deficiencies to avoid customer dissatisfaction.

Juran's Quality Trilogy

Juran focused on three major quality processes, known as the Quality Trilogy (Juran, 1989):

1. Quality planning involves developing the products, systems and processes needed to meet or exceed customer expectations. It should determine who the customers are, identify customer needs, develop products with features according to customer needs, develop systems and processes that allow the organisation to produce these features and deploy the plans to operational level.
2. Quality control involves assessing actual quality performance, comparing performance with goals and acting on differences between performance and goals.
3. Quality improvement should be ongoing and continual, and requires the development of infrastructures necessary to achieve annual quality improvements; identify specific areas in need of improvement; implement improvement projects; establish a team with the responsibility of completing each improvement project; and provide teams with what they need to be able to diagnose problems to determine root causes, develop solutions and controls that will maintain gains made.

I believe that this trilogy of Juran's is very important for quality; but it needs a continual learning and co-creating culture to go with it, in addition to the development of skills through training and continual learning.

Stephen Uselac (1993) states that: 'Juran favours the concept of quality circles because they improve communication between management and labour. Furthermore, he recommends the use of statistical process control, but does believe that quality is not free. He explains that within the law of diminishing returns, quality will optimise, and beyond that point conformance is more costly than the value of the quality obtained.'

Juran's Quality Planning Road Map, consists of the following steps (Rampersad, 2005, pp. 6–7):

1. Identify who are the customers.
2. Determine the needs of those customers.
3. Translate those needs into our language.
4. Develop a product that can respond to those needs.
5. Optimise the product features, so as to meet those needs.
6. Optimise the product features so as to meet our needs as well as customer needs.
7. Develop a process which is able to produce the product.
8. Optimise the process.
9. Prove that the process can produce the product under operating conditions.
10. Transfer the process to operation.

Juran's and Deming's philosophies have many similar aspects. The focus on top management, the need for improvement, the use of quality control techniques and the importance of training are fundamental to both philosophies.

We must now go to Japan to become acquainted with other notable figures in the quality arena, including Kaoru Ishikawa and Genichi Taguchi.

Kaoru Ishikawa (ASQC, 1986)

An early pioneer in the quality revolution in Japan, Kaoru Ishikawa, was the foremost figure in Japanese quality until his death in 1989. He was instrumental in the development of the broad outlines of Japanese quality strategy. Dr Ishikawa was a professor of engineering at Tokyo University for many years. He was also a member of the editorial review board of the Japanese journal *Quality Control for Foremen*, founded in 1962, and later the Chief Executive Director of the Quality Control Circle Headquarters at the Union of Japanese Scientists and Engineers (JUSE). Dr Ishikawa influenced the development of a participative, bottom-up view of quality that became the trademark of the Japanese approach to quality management. He persuaded the Japanese that a company-wide approach to quality control was necessary for total success. Ishikawa built and promoted greater involvement from senior management than from front-line staff, and reduced reliance on quality professionals and quality departments. He advocated the collection and analysis of factual data using simple visual tools, statistical techniques and teamwork as the foundation for implementing TQ. Like others, Ishikawa believed that quality begins with the customer, and therefore understanding customer needs is the basis for improvement. He felt that complaints should be actively sought. The elements of his philosophy are ten points as follows:

- Quality begins with education and ends with education.
- The first step in quality is to know the requirements of customers.
- The ideal state of quality control occurs when inspection is no longer necessary.
- Remove the root cause, not the symptoms.
- Quality control is the responsibility of all workers and all divisions.
- Do not confuse the means with the objectives.
- Put quality first and set your sights on long-term profits.

- Marketing is the entrance and exit of quality.
- Top management must not show anger when facts are presented by subordinates.
- Ninety-five per cent of problems in a company can be solved with simple tools for analysis and problem solving. Data without dispersion is false data.

Ishikawa wanted to change the way people think about work (Ishikawa, 1985). He urged managers to resist becoming content with merely improving a product's quality, insisting that quality improvement can always go one step further. His notion of company-wide quality, in addition to his 10 points, called for continued customer service. This meant that a customer would continue to receive service even after receiving the product. This service would extend across the company itself, at all levels of management, and even beyond the company, to the everyday lives of those involved. According to Ishikawa, quality improvement is a continuous process and can always be taken one step further.

With his cause-and-effect diagram (also called the 'Ishikawa' or 'fishbone' diagram) Ishikawa made significant and specific advancements in quality improvement. By using this diagram, the user can see all possible causes of a result and, hopefully, find the root of process imperfections. By pin-pointing root problems, the diagram provides quality improvement from the 'bottom up'. Deming adopted the diagram and used it to teach TQC in Japan as early as the Second World War. Both Ishikawa and Deming used this same diagram as one the first tools in the quality management process.

Ishikawa also showed the importance of the six quality tools: control chart, run chart, histogram, scatter diagram, Pareto chart, and flowchart. Additionally, he explored the concept of quality circles as a Japanese philosophy that he brought out from obscurity to world-wide acceptance. Ishikawa believed in the importance of support and leadership from senior management. He continually urged senior executives to take quality-control courses, knowing that, without the support of management, these programmes would ultimately fail. He stressed that it would take firm commitment from the entire hierarchy of employees to reach the company's potential for success. Another area of quality improvement that Ishikawa emphasised was quality throughout a product's life cycle – not just during production.

Although he believed firmly in creating standards, he felt that standards were like continuous quality-improvement programmes, and that they too should be constantly evaluated and changed. Standards are not the ultimate source of decision making; customer satisfaction is. He wanted managers to consistently meet consumer needs; from these needs, all other decisions should stem. Besides his own developments, Ishikawa drew on and expounded on the principles of other quality leaders, including Deming, the creator of the Plan-Do-Check-Act-Analyse model. He expanded Deming's four steps into the following six (Figure 5.4):

1. Determine goals and targets.
2. Determine methods of reaching goals.
3. Engage in education and training.
4. Implement work.
5. Check the effects of implementation.
6. Take appropriate action.

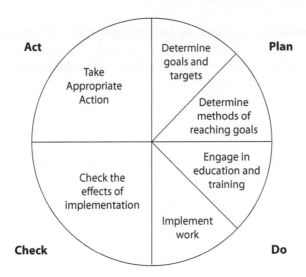

Figure 5.4   Ishikawa model (plan, do, check, act)

Genichi Taguchi

Genichi Taguchi, a Japanese engineer whose philosophy was advocated by Deming, explained the economic value of reducing variation. Taguchi maintained that the manufacturing-based definition of quality, as conformance to specification limits, is inherently flawed. He measured quality as the variation from the target value of design specification and then translated that variation into an economic 'loss function' that expresses the cost of variation in monetary terms.

Taguchi focused his methodology on testing products prior to the manufacturing process. This is a prototyping method that enables the designer to identify the optimal settings to produce a robust product, by breaking down off-line quality control into three stages: system design, parameter design and tolerance design.

Through these thinkers, the implementation of TQM in Japan, together with Japanese ideology, led to great success in economics and all other walks of life. The Japanese achieved great progress in all disciplines during the 1970s and 1980s; and Japan was competitive in many disciplines world-wide, and not just at home.

Japanese excellence in business propelled policy makers and businessmen in America to examine the underlying causes of this excellence and to ask why, if Japan was able to achieve excellence, they were not. Extensive efforts and intensive research projects were undertaken to solve this problem. The findings revealed that Japanese success was due to the nature of the Japanese management model.

The dimensions of the model were pin-pointed and analysed and it was verified that the Japanese had adopted the TQM approach or system. Western enterprises and organisations adopted the TQM system and tried to identify the system's components for successful implementation in practice.

They realised that the TQM system was not fragmented, nor just a technical document to be introduced and built into the organisation without any integrative effort. It was thus recognised as an integrated system or total system. Moreover, management philosophy characterises the model as a totality. All the findings of Western research and studies on the model were essentially retrospective and narrative. No empirical or comprehensive research was conducted to study the essence of the TQM philosophy and the conditions for its implementation in the West..

Conclusion

In the Arab world, the end result of such theories and conceptual contributions has been mixed. To some extent they have enhanced the foundations of our organisations, introducing systems and processes that have given stability to public and private enterprises.

However, such quality approaches generally, and TQM specifically, have been imposed from the outside, without due consideration for our own values and context. In other words, the approach has been global–local, rather than local–global, outside-in rather than inside-out. All too often, then, disabled, impractical and inapplicable, the approach has been fragmented.

Japanese thinkers on TQ, Ishikawa and Taguchi, started with their own, local Japanese spirit, and added to it Western technique from the likes of Deming and Juran. As a result, the implementation of TQ in Japan has met with great success, at least in the 1970s and 1980s. But in the Arab world, where is the Islamic philosophy in all of this?

An Islamic philosophy is needed, because neither the Western theory nor the Japanese theory can be implemented in the context of an Islamic culture. The Islamic theory of management, as we shall soon see, is based on the unification (*Al-Tawheed*) of objectives among workers, senior management (or owners) and society. *Al-Tawheed* is the unification (totally and partially) of contradictions, such as individual and group. We need a theory that is based on religion and faith and accompanied by a values system whereby compliance with and implementation of the theory becomes a religious practice and *Itqan* is seen as a form of worship. With justice as the core value in Islam, I.Theory's concepts and the total view of values are exemplified both within and outside the organisation, as we shall see in the following chapters.

In the next chapter I shall discuss important Islamic philosophers and how the Islamic state implemented quality control systems in all the major Islamic institutions in the past. This is followed by a comparison with modern quality management systems, such as ISO 9001.

CHAPTER 6 *Quality in Islam*

Introduction

HISBA AND DAWAWEEN

In the previous chapter I reviewed the mainstream literature on quality in America and Japan, from a management perspective. Prior to this, I argued that if we are to align quality with transformation, in our Arab context, we need to evolve local identity towards global integrity, rather than thinking globally (in this case American or Japanese) and acting locally within the Arab world. I will start this chapter by taking up where I left off in Chapter 1 and reviewing the approach to quality (*Itqan*) in Islam – in practice and in theory – based on the holy Qur'an and the commentaries (Sunnah), before moving on to I.Theory.

I will focus, to begin with, on *Shura* (consultation) and other similar Islamic values, using two main approaches, the so-called *Hisba* system (quality control) and the *Dawaween* system (management information control system). I will explain the main functions of the *Al-Hisba* system that was applied by *Al-Muhtasib* (the Inspector). The *Al-Dawaween* system is related to documentation as a major element in management communication throughout Islamic states. I will also discuss how, according to Hisham Sharabi (Al-Sharabi, 1988), colonialism created a patriarchal system in the Islamic and Arab worlds, whereby freedoms, including the freedom of thought and expression, were constricted, with grave ramifications for society.

ORIENTATION TO I.THEORY

There is no doubt that management, as a phenomenon, is considered a distinct domain, established implicitly rather than explicitly, when the first human being was created. Management taxonomies are a human phenomenon, reflecting rational humanity in a relational manner, including (wo)man's relationship with her- or himself, her/his family, life around her/him, her/ his organisation and/or society. (Wo)man practised all these relationship without using 'management', as an explicit expression, until the nineteenth century, when human thought, especially in America, began to perceive the special and distinguishing character of management as an independent phenomenon.

However, as management research ensued, management was identified, in a partial way, as an effort, an activity, a tool, a system and/or a process, rather than an evolution of human relatedness. It is therefore necessary to look at management as a human phenomenon; and in that light it needs to be further clarified and defined. This is where, in an Islamic context, I.Theory comes in, paying great attention to the human element in management. But in order to fully understand this theory as compared with other management theories, we need first to explore quality in Islam in general.

Quality in Islam

ITQAN AND SHURA

The philosophical context of quality in Islam stems from the holy Qur'an and the Sunnah (the teachings of Mohammad, the Prophet of Islam, Peace be upon him). As will be discussed below, Islamic principles reinforce and enhance quality in management, which is a substantial element in achieving *Itqan* (a quality-related term used by Prophet Mohammad to denote continually improving performance by the parties in any task, activity or function).

Shura, as we have seen, is a quality term used in the Qur'an in *Sura Al-Shura* (The Consultation), *aya* 88: '*And their matters are attained by consultation between them.*' *Shura* emphasises teamwork and cohesion among members of the group in Islamic society, for the purpose of empowering groups and society.

Allah asks us to achieve *Itqan*, as indicated in *Sura Al-Namel* (The Ants), *aya* 38: '*It is the nature of Allah to perfect everything.*' The Qur'an condemns all deception in daily dealings as well as, and especially, in all matters of religion and daily life. In several *ayas* (1–5) of *Sura Al-Mutaffiffeen* (The Cheaters), Allah says: '*Woe to those that deal in fraud, those who, where they have to receive by measure from men, exact full measure, but when they have to give by measure or weight to men, give less than due. Do they not think that they will be raised up on a Mighty Day.*'

Prophet Mohammad said: '*You are not a believer of Allah, unless you like for your brother what you like for yourself*' (*Saheeh Bukhari* and *Saheeh Muslim*). This emphasises the crucial sense of community and selflessness, among members, organisations and society as whole, for the achievement equity, equality and social integration.

Moreover, Prophet Mohammad asked us to act responsibly in holding any position or performing our jobs and duties. In his saying '*All of you are providers of care and everybody is responsible to do it right for his subordinates and dependents*' (Saheeh Bukhari and Muslim), he explains that we all have responsibilities, whether in the family, in the workplace or in society as a whole. These responsibilities towards ourselves and others mean that we should be honest, transparent and just, through the following approaches (Al-Sheikh, 2000):

1. To draw from the perfection of Allah's work ('*And be good, as God has been good to you. And do not seek corruption on earth, for God does not love the corrupt*' [*Aya* 77, *sura* Alqasas]).
2. To follow the best standards ('*And follow the best of what has been revealed to you from your God.*' [*Aya* 55, *sura* Alzumor]).
3. To uphold ethics within a value system that governs society.
4. To have excellence (Prophet Mohammad said, '*Do the best as if you see Allah, if not, Allah sees you.*' [Saheeh Bukhari]).
5. To ensure integration in any task and behaviour.

TOTAL QUALITY IN ISLAM

In his book *Total Quality in Islam*, Al-Sheikh summarises what good work (religious, professional, social) in Islam means, and indicates that it should have the following five principles:

1. *Integration among all aspects of work* (the objectives and techniques) – worship is not complete without good deeds.
2. Good work is not only doing good but avoiding the bad and *keeping self and others safe* from harm as well.
3. Good work should be both ethical and successful.
4. The utility of work, which means that any work should benefit the worker, such as welfare, a *good social life and health.*
5. Preparation and training to do good work, which requires *effort and knowledge.*

The Islamic system was based on individual self-actualisation, which means allowing individuals to reach the peak – *Itqan* – in the performance of their duties. A system was created to fit the people and the activity involved, not the other way around (i.e. creating a system and fitting people into it). This is what I have tried to create in this book, as my contribution to filling the gap in management theories and putting Islamic theory into practice.

ISLAMIC PHILOSOPHERS ON QUALITY AND ETHICS

Many Muslim scholars have touched on aspects of work ethics and regulation to clarify and explain the Qur'an and Sunnah in relation to quality and good work.

Abu al-Hassan al-Mawardi: ethics and jurisprudence

Abu al-Hassan al-Mawardi was an Arab Muslim jurist. He made contributions to Qur'anic interpretations, philology, ethics and literature. He was born in Basrah in Iraq (972–1058 CE). He wrote several books in political science and sociology, like *Al-Ahkam al-Sultania wal-Wilayat al-Diniyya* (The Ordinances of Government) and *Kitab Aadab al-Dunya wal Din* (The Ethics of Religion and World Affairs).

Ibn Taymiyah, Taqi al-Din Abu al-Abbas: Following the Righteous Path

Ibn Taymiyah, Taqi al-Din Abu al-Abbas (1263–1323 CE) was a Muslim scholar born in Harran, located in what is now Turkey. He held that much of the Islamic scholarship of his time had declined into modes that were inherently against the proper understanding of the Qur'an and the Sunnah. He strove to:

- revive the Islamic faith's understanding of 'true' adherence to *Tawheed*
- eradicate beliefs and customs that he held to be foreign to Islam, and
- rejuvenate correct Islamic thought and its related sciences and systems such as *Al Hisbah* (Quality Control).

In his book *Kitab Iqtida al-Sirat al-Mustaqim* (On Following the Righteous Path), Ibn Taymiyah maintained that the first three generations of Muslims were the best role models for Islamic life. In his book *Al-Jihad*, he answered and explained all questions put to him relating to the Qur'an and Sunnah, and covered such dimensions in life (Aljazar, 1998).

Abu Hamid Al-Ghazali: towards the perfect market

Abu Hamid Al-Ghazali (1058–1111 CE) was one of the greatest Islamic jurists, theologians and mystical thinkers. He was appointed head of the Nizamiyyah College in Baghdad in 1091. In Book 1 of his series of volumes *Ihiya' Oloum Al-Deen* (Revival of Religious Sciences), Abu Hamid Al-Ghazali defined the criteria of the perfect market in Islam as follows:

- Free from monopoly.
- Free from fraud or under-standardised commodities with defects (promoting such material is forbidden).
- Equitable and fair prices.
- Prudent behaviour by purchasers and merchandisers or traders (to be honest and fair in any deal).
- Transparent dealings with no deception – with forgiveness being the rule.
- Any dealing in forbidden commodities or materials banned by the controller (*Al-Muhtaseb*) is considered illegal. The *Al-Muhtaseb* is also responsible for assuring compliance with the above criteria and standards. The *Al-Muhtaseb* issues penalties in cases of deviation from the approved standards.

Al-Shizary: the end does not justify the means

Al-Shizary, a twelfth-century Muslim scholar, indicated that the *Al Muhtaseb* or his deputy, as a quality inspector, must be knowledgeable in Islamic legislation and jurisdiction, in addition to being a *Faqih* (scholar in Islamic teachings), in order to be able to make informed decisions regarding what people need to do or avoid. The philosophy of the end justifying the means is forbidden by Islamic ethical standards. Any person who follows this principle must be punished because it is contrary to Islamic teachings. By contrast, honourable principles call for righteousness, equality and beneficence. The qualifications set for the *Al-Muhtaseb* established very high criteria. They required the *Al-Muhtaseb* to work within his knowledge and job description, to appreciate the limitations of his duties and consult with other legislators, and to practise what he preached (Al-Daher, 1997).

All of the above and many other philosophers have explored values, ethics and the standards of good work as a kind of quality. We now turn to quality control, and specifically to self-control, in Islam.

SELF-CONTROL IN ISLAM

One of the important fundamentals of quality control and management in Islam is self-control, which is exemplified by internal and external control at the level of the self, family, organisation, management and all the way up to the level of the state. All the foregoing quality and ethical considerations aim to ensure that previously planned objectives and functions are performed according to Islamic theology and law, which are gleaned from the holy Qur'an and the Sunnah. Instilling values in the individual, in Islam as in other religions and doctrines, begins from birth. The process of acquiring values needs to begin at a very early stage in order for those values to become intrinsic to the person. A very important value that needs to be ingrained in people from childhood, and that will be reflected later on in their personal and professional life and exercise of other values, is self-control and self-monitoring. For an organisation, this means that individual will be able to perform their work with *Itqan* without much external control.

It is not possible to discuss all aspects related to quality in Islam in this book. I will focus on those related to organisational management, including two major taxonomies in achieving quality, which can be summarised as the two main systems, as already mentioned: *Al-Hisba* (quality control) and the *Dawaween* (bureaucratic control) system. These systems are equivalent to what we now call 'management information and control systems' and were applied in government ministries and in official institutions in former Islamic eras. We start with *Al-Hisba*.

Al-Hisba System (Quality Control System)

A FAITH-BASED MISSION

The philosophy of *Hisba* (Al-Baqmi, 1995) as a quality control system has its roots in the holy Qur'an. Many *ayas* urge people to be righteous and to lead by example in order to perpetuate a culture of righteousness. In *aya* 44 of *Sura Al-Baqara* (The Cow), Allah says: *'Do you order people to be pious while forgetting yourselves, even though you read the book? Do you not understand?'*

The purpose of *Al-Hisba* is to prevent any deviation (Islamic standards being the reference point) from a required standard, adding value and hindering corruption so as to safeguard individuals and society as a whole from tort or any obstacles that might challenge the ultimate goal of improving the quality of life for everyone. It covers all aspects of life: industry, agriculture, trade and any other services.

The *Al-Hisba* philosophy is basically a faith-based mission. It was developed mainly as a management control system to control institutions and businesses in the Islamic state. The primary goal of the *Al-Hisba* system is the prevention of corruption, deviation and any other illicit behaviour in institutions.

INTRODUCING AL-MUHTASEB

In order to administer the *Al-Hisba* system, the position of *Al-Muhtaseb* was introduced. The *Al-Muhtaseb* in Islamic management culture is equivalent to the general performance inspector. It was considered a high-ranking position, similar to that of a judge today. In early Islam, during Prophet Mohammad's times, state governors employed the *Al-Muhtaseb* to exercise control over state institutions and departments.

The *Al-Muhtaseb* was an independent inspector and controller assigned by the caliph (ruler of the state in Islam). He had full authority to control the performance of state organisations and workers in any field, and had the right to take appropriate disciplinary action.

The *Al-Muhtaseb* must be transparent. His intentions must be congruent with his actions. He must avoid conflict of interest, avoid abusing his position and avoid any competition with others for self-serving purposes.

The *Al-Muhtaseb* must have initiative, honesty and the ability to influence people to follow the right path. A code of ethics requires the *Al-Muhtaseb* to take an oath by which he commits himself to follow Islamic standards, ethics and norms. Moreover, he must uphold the rights of the people, the state and the council of state or government. The oath also required the *Al-Muhtaseb* to perform his work with honesty and loyalty and in co-operation with the organisation, as if he were a staff member. In terms of demeanour, he must be friendly and amicable in his leadership, communications and directions, and avoid cruel behaviour under any circumstances.

The main functions of *Al-Hisba* that must be performed by the *Al-Muhtaseb*, in the arena of management in Islam with which we are concerned, were the following:

- Controlling markets and roads to *ensure compliance* with the building codes.
- *Controlling the standards* of craftsmen and manual workers by appointing specialists from each domain of industry or service to act as inspectors for the assigned discipline and assure compliance with the standards of the industry or profession. For example, a specialised *Muhtaseb* was assigned to inspect tailors, textile workers, painters, shoemakers or goldsmiths.
- *Inspecting measurements*, such as those of textiles, and assuring standardisation of all measurements and commodities.
- Controlling brokers in markets to *prevent any deception* by emphasising honesty and transparency in the selling and buying of goods and commodities.
- *Controlling the performance* of teachers and Kutab (teachers of Qur'an, Arabic, Sunnah and Fiqh – Islamic affairs, business, Islamic culture and sciences).
- Exercising control over governors, princes of states, judges and attorneys by monitoring their performance and *urging them to be righteous* and abstain from any misconduct (e.g. bribery or corruption).

As is evident from the above, the *Hisba* system exercised a form of centralised control over all state processes and institutions. This can be seen as an advantage because it meant integration and harmony in control systems and efforts. Nowadays in most Islamic states there are control systems that can be viewed as modern versions of the *Hisba* SYSTEM; however, these bodies have all too often been overtaken by unduly bureaucratic, or indeed autocratic, systems and processes, precluding self-control. We now turn to *Al-Dawaween*.

Al-Dawaween System (Information Management and Control Systems in Islam)

WRITING AS A CORE ELEMENT IN LIFE

The development of *Dawaween* systems is linked primarily with the development of the printing industry, particularly the printing of *Dawaween*, which was adopted from the time of the emergence of the Islamic state until the present. Writing was considered a core element in life. The *Dawaween* were concerned with gathering and sorting documents and verifying their accuracy and precision, in addition to the retrieval, dissemination and management of state-related correspondence.

Functional documentation of communications was not, in fact, a priority as such. Administrators concentrated on creative writing as a tool for intellectual, scientific and literary communication in order to document and spread knowledge and information.

Writing, then, played a significant role in establishing *Dawaween* systems or the *Diwan*, which was viewed in those days as a means of public administration or bureaucracy. It was a form of bureaucratic quality control system. Writing was the chief medium for information exchange and communication both in and among different *Dawaween* (bureaus) in the court of the caliphate (*Bait Al-Khilafa*), in administration offices, in the treasury (*Bait Al-Mal*), in different provinces of the state and among citizens. The most prominent features of *Dawaween* can be summarised as follows:

1. The development of a coding system to organise archives and facilitate document retrieval.
2. *Kitaba* (writing) denoted the performance of office tasks and scientific actions, and record keeping, including the keeping of ledgers, particularly in *Dawaween* duties and tasks.

Meanwhile, *Kitaba* writing spread in all states. Since the Arabic language was considered the language of the Qur'an, it became the language of communication, documentation and management in administering the affairs of the Islamic Arab state. Essays and letters directed people to embrace Islam, and all treaty agreements and the authentication of treaties and declarations were confirmed by documents.

WRITING AND DOCUMENTATION

The work of *Dawaween* started in the early years of the *Hijra*, when Prophet Mohammad emigrated from Mecca to Medina and established the Islamic state. Realising the importance of documenting knowledge, Prophet Mohammad instructed Muslims to learn how to write. Writing became a major method for *Da'wa* (the call to Islam).

An important *Diwan* was the *Diwan* of Issuance. It was a kind of a central *Diwan* for all state affairs. The *Diwan* included more than 30 writers, copyists and interpreters. *Kutab Al-Wahi* (writers of the revelation) were responsible for writing down the revealed *suras* and *ayas* (chapters and verses), as directed by Prophet Mohammad. There were also correspondence, financial, military and census writers.

ESTABLISHMENT OF INTEGRATED DAWAWEEN SYSTEMS

Integrated *Dawaween* systems (bureaucratic systems) were established during the rule of Caliph Omar Bin Al-Khattab (Al-Hasaniya, 1997) in the seventh century CE. Before his time, the *Dawaween* were not organised or integrated in their documentation of management and financial affairs but, with the huge expansion of the Islamic state, the need arose for more integrated and better organised systems.

As a natural result of the expansion of the state, state institutions and bodies also grew and expanded, , in particular, the army. Revenues increased, and with them expenses.

Dawaween were therefore evolved as management control and quality control systems to control the huge state. The main *Dawaween*s at the time included the *Diwan Al-Rasael* (correspondence bureau), the *Diwan Al-Isdar* (issuance bureau), the military bureau and the *Diwan Al-Ata'* (grants bureau).

During the Umayyad era, from the death of the Prophet in 632 CE until 1031 CE, the systems of *Dawaween* were enlarged and extended to include all categories of work and businesses. What characterised these *Dawaween*s was that they were multilingual, using Arabic, Persian and Latin. Writing and the *Dawaween* industry witnessed further expansion during the Abbasid era. During this period there was great interest in and state patronage of the arts and sciences. Baghdad was a centre of trade, including in books.

With the decline of Muslim civilisation from the fourteenth to the twentieth centuries CE, the 'quality' culture of systematic documentation and control, running alongside a culture of intellectual attainment and scientific curiosity, declined into bureaucracy, autocracy and corrupt practice.

NEO-PATRIARCHY: THE FALL OF THE OTTOMAN EMPIRE AND THE RISE OF THE MODERN ERA

After the fall of the Ottoman Empire, Arab Islamic states came under colonial influence and control. The best analysis of the socio-political state of the Arab world during the course of the twentieth century has been provided by Dr Hisham Al-Sharabi in his book on *Neo-patriarchy* (Al-Sharabi, 1988). He maintained that, over the course of the twentieth century, Arab society became governed by the systems of patriarchy and dependency, giving rise to a particular form of socio-political structure that can be described as a neo-patriarchal system and is characterised by:

1. Social fragmentation: the family, clan, religion or ethnic group, rather than the nation or civic society, constitutes the basis of social relations and corresponding social organisation.
2. Authoritarian organisation: domination, coercion and paternalism, rather than co-operation, mutual recognition and equality, govern all relations, from the micro-structure of the family to the macro-structure of the state.
3. Absolutist paradigms: a closed, absolutist consciousness in theoretical practice, in politics and in everyday life, grounded in transcendence, metaphysics, revelation and closure.
4. Ritualistic practice: behaviour governed by ceremony, customs and ritual, rather than by spontaneity, creativity and innovation.

In other words, Al-Sharabi indicates that the tradition of system, documentation, self-control and quality control has not been updated and evolved through a healthy interaction between tradition and modernity. Rather, he claims, an unhealthy fusion has occurred, inhibiting the freedom of the individual within the community. Instead, we have the restrictive authority of family and clan, on the one hand, and of a bureaucratic system, on the other.

As we can see, just as the door of *Ijtihad* (interpretation of Islamic law) was closed in the seventh century CE, the notion of quality has not been continually evolving in the Arab world. For Sardar, 'They have also ignored the future-oriented message of their faith

– the very source of the dynamism inherent in Muslim civilisation. As a result, Muslim understanding of the worldview of Islam has been frozen in history' (Sardar, 2006). For Al-Sharabi, neo-patriarchy is a phenomenon seen not only in families: it can be seen in the modern form of the state in the Islamic world, which he called the 'neo-sultanate'.

Conclusion

Casting our minds back to the previous chapter, we can see the principle of TQM today as an evolution of the *Hisba* and *Dawaween* systems that existed centuries ago in the Arab and Islamic worlds. Moreover, when Islamic civilisation was at its height, not only were systematic documentation and purposeful quality control clearly in evidence; they were also closely aligned with a culture that promoted the retrieval, sharing and indeed creation of knowledge (*Itqan*). In other words, and in today's managerial terms, total quality, organisational learning and knowledge creation were duly aligned.

The fact that TQ has been imported wholesale from the West (America) and the East (Japan) means that such a process of renewal and integration has not taken place. Our purpose in developing and implementing I.Theory is to help bring that about. In Chapter 7 we will turn to this, comparing and contrasting I.Theory (justice), with the prevailing management philosophies of America (efficiency) and Japan (equality).

7 *Comparative Management Philosophy: An Initial Outline*

Introduction

MANAGEMENT BY SUFFICIENCY, EFFICIENCY AND EFFECTIVENESS

Now that I have introduced you to a historically evolved, Islamic approach to quality, to be compared and contrasted with the conventional American and Japanese one, it is time to broaden out from quality, specifically, to management, generally. I now want to compare the development of management philosophies prior to the industrial age. I term these management by sufficiency, management by efficiency and management by effectiveness, the latter being represented by our 'I.Theory', which is based on the unification of objectives and continual improvement, in Islamic terms. The approach in this chapter will be very general. I will then go into more detail in Chapter 8.

Stages of Management Development

The stages of development of management philosophy are as follows:

FIRST STAGE: PAROCHIAL MANAGEMENT: T/TRADITIONAL MODEL

This is embodied in parochial societies, which do not have codified institutions. The model has no ultimate core values. In fact, a parochial mode that exhibits incoherence and special, individual interests is an idiosyncratic system.

SECOND STAGE: MANAGEMENT BY SUFFICIENCY: L1/LIBERAL MODEL[1] US MODEL

This model is based on regulations and laws, such as scientific management or Taylor's theory (Taylor, 1911) and Henry Fayol's (Fayol, 1981) organisational theory. This was the first revolution in management, because all its theories focused on institutional building. To organise institutions, management must implement laws and regulations and employees should follow them. Thus, management by laws (MBL) emerged, which

---

1   L1 is a symbol for the liberal model in the USA in the early decades of the twentieth century.

is synonymous with management by sufficiency, which aims at the enhancement of productivity. All workers follow laws and regulations to the letter. With this model, we see the following results:

- The management system is centralised.
- Laws and regulations are not the core value, but the sufficiency value is central to achieving organisational objectives.
- Relations between the management and employees are controlled by the power of law, with no opportunity for discussion or negotiation.

Moreover, with MBL, workers are required to perform their set functions, without any continual increase or decrease in productivity. This is the old version of ISO 9000, issued by the International Organization for Standardization (ISO)in 1987 and 1994. This means that with the old version of ISO 9000, the world moved backwards by 100 years. For Seddon (Seddon, 1997), the emphasis tended to be placed on conformity with procedures rather than on the overall process of management. These standards were generalised worldwide until 2000, when, in a major step towards TQM, the ISO issued an updated standard. ISO 9001:2000 sought to bring about a radical change in thinking by actually placing the concept of process management to the fore and centre ('process management' was monitoring and optimising of the company's tasks and activities, instead of just inspecting the final product). ISO 9001:2000 also demands the involvement of senior executives, and expects continual process improvement and tracking of customer satisfaction.

THIRD STAGE: MANAGEMENT BY EFFICIENCY: L2/LIBERAL MODEL[2] US MODEL

This model is based on a core value of efficiency in performance (high quality, maximum quantity, less cost and less time). It takes into consideration what senior management wants its employees to follow, but has some room for initiatives to improve performance and levels of productivity. This is similar to ISO 9001:2000, issued in the year 2000, but these clauses are linked to quality objectives in the organisation. The transformation to this stage occurred in the USA and other Western societies in the mid-1930s.

Laws are enacted as a means of organising all relationships pertaining to society and organisations. The transformation here was that management developed the concept of laws and helped employees to achieve their objectives. Emphasis was not limited to laws and implementation, but was also placed on the significance of having more freedom.

People are urged to use their initiative and self-motivation to improve their performance in all aspects (quantity, quality, time, place and cost), to transform in view of a law (a behavioural standard) and to view it as an organising tool. Therefore, management was transformed from management by efficiency and management by laws to management by objectives (MBO). Management by efficiency does not deal with employees as a power inside the organisation, but sees them as a tool for productivity. We can see the following results:

---

2   L2 is a symbol for the liberal model in the USA after Hawthorn's experiments in the mid-1930s.

1. The fundamental philosophy is one of initiative, which must be in harmony with the philosophy of efficiency. Thus, the nature of management is decentralised, and is human.
2. In the Western liberal management model, the initiative of employees depends on the philosophy of competition in all activities. The philosophy of organisation is efficiency of productivity, the philosophy of management is efficiency of performance and the philosophy of employees is one of initiative.

Duncan (1999) stated in Chapter 3 of his book *Management Ideas and Actions*: 'If there is one word linked with management in people's minds, it is Efficiency.' The scientific management movement is called management by efficiency. But when we study scientific management, it concentrates on how to achieve efficient productivity, that is, organisational authority. Duncan alternates between efficiency and sufficiency.

It is obvious that such as company is based on regulations and laws more than on human arrangements. It is consistent with 'sufficiency' more than efficiency. Of course, regulations and instructions are very important for achieving organisational objectives. However, they are not the basis for identifying the philosophy of management and its ultimate core value. This philosophy is based on the nature of relations between management and employees. This is the core difference, which has not been mentioned in the standard approach to Western management until now, even though the Human Relations movement of the 1950s and 1960s tried to address it, without lasting or sustainable effect.

So neither a sufficiency orientation nor an efficiency orientation has adopted quality and transformation to achieve continual improvement as a philosophy of management.

FOURTH STAGE: MANAGEMENT BY EFFECTIVENESS: JAPANESE MODEL, ISLAMIC MODEL

This stage has not yet been fully addressed, which is why this book has been written. There is a lack of clarity about its nature and scope, and this affects efforts to build it up as the most evolved model.

There is some contemporary experience of this model, such as the Japanese and German models. Moreover, some American companies, such as Interface in Atlanta, which has a strong environmental and social orientation, are searching for a new managerial philosophy that differs from previous ones. They are trying to build a managerial model that complies with quality in the round; however, it is impossible to build any political or managerial model that is fundamentally transformative without first basing it on a philosophy that arises from an ultimate value.

I believe that the sufficiency and efficiency models are not ideal. There are no ultimate values therein for realising a unified ultimate vision that satisfies all parties in organisational life. To be unified, generalised and ideal, a model must be able to secure unified objectives and interests, whereby all parties, both within the organisation and outside it, are fully represented. Thereby:

- owners secure productivity, efficiency, and maximisation of profit
- employees gain welfare and happiness, and
- society at large partakes in civilisational development.

Figure 7.1   Objective triangle

For Assaf (2005), two elements are required to implement this model:

1. Unification between organisational and employee objectives means the organisation is no better than its employees. Senior management must genuinely consider employees as an asset, not only as a resource. On the other hand, this philosophy emphasises co-operation between employees, without the conflict or competition that destroys the organisation.
2. Unification between organisational and societal objectives, whereby organisations have social responsibility.

I see the results of this effectiveness orientation, firstly, as follows:

- The important value for establishing positive relationships is co-operation, over and above competition.
- Employees must participate in setting goals and developing strategies.
- Social responsibility must be exercised integrally, not as a mere add-on.

Secondly, three basic requirements are involved in the ongoing development of organisations, now and in the future.

- Initiative, which involves individuals' self-energy in relationship with others, thereby unifying subject and object for mutual benefit.
- Innovation: This implies individual mental energy and reflects the human factor. It emphasises innovation in both the psychological and social aspects of enterprise.
- Creation: This focuses on individuals' technical energy and ingenuity, which is different from social innovation. It is correlated with idea–reality or knowledge–skills: there is no creation without innovation.

To put these objectives into a unified perspective, they can be summarised as a core, ultimate value, or core reality. Here, the concept of effectiveness is the most appropriate. I see the science of management, integrally speaking, as the science of effectiveness.

Any management that adopts the philosophy of effectiveness assumes an ultimate value that has a unifying characteristic, i.e. it unites everyone in a common goal (authority's interests and objectives, co-workers' interests and objectives, society's interests and objectives). This may lead us to consider this value as an ultimate core value. Two basic assumptions will help us to understand 'I.Theory' in relation to this value:

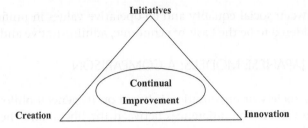

Figure 7.2   The continual improvement triangle

- There are some specific cultural conditions within the organisation that underlie management by effectiveness.
- These conditions must be in tune with the larger, societal culture, as in feel locally, think locally–globally and act locally.

We will now conclude by comparing and contrasting the Anglo-Saxon and Japanese models.

Conclusion

THE WESTERN MODEL – MARKET FREEDOM

Prior to the Industrial Revolution, Western societies were under centralised control. The Industrial Revolution emphasised freedom, which is correlated with democracy, as a core value in these societies. However, the elite and the aristocracy (political or economic) continued to have economic power, leading them to control society.

Meanwhile, management theory developed, and concentrated, in effect, on the efficiency dimension, notwithstanding attempts to establish 'humanistic' approaches to management. The transformation towards freedom took place politically and economically, from a market and consumer perspective, but not from an employee perspective – except insofar as a person might be free to choose the employer for whom to work, or to pursue self-employment if able to take that risk.

THE JAPANESE MODEL – EMPLOYER/EMPLOYEE EQUALITY

The Japanese experience of management started in the mid-1960s with the search for a philosophical identity, economically and managerially, leading to the unification of the country. This identity was based on indigenous values, which brought dignity to society. Those in power and the senior management in Japan did not see freedom as an ultimate core value, as was the case in the West. The West was already developed, and there was a gap between Japan and the West. In Japan the senior management[3] chose social equality as an ultimate core value, which is necessary as a foundation for building all vertical and horizontal relationships.

---

3   Emperor Migi adopted this philosophy from Nietzsche.

Harmony between social equality and co-operative values in unified and integrated systems was considered to be the basis of economic, administrative and political systems.

WESTERN AND JAPANESE MODELS: A COMPARISON

The power of any society or organisation is based on its general philosophy and values, especially its core values. The differences between the liberal and the Japanese models are as follows. The two models have distinct philosophical aspects. These include aspects of the philosophical system, society, organisation and management. Western culture and civilisation adopted the value of freedom in its liberal system. Japan adopted social equality and co-operative values, and enhanced those values through its general educational system.

The main differences between the two philosophies are as follows:

1. The individual is the basis of the Western philosophy, particularly in American society, while the group is the basis and the focus of Japanese philosophy.
2. The basic values in Western society are conflict and competition (survival of the fittest). There is minimal opportunity for teamwork or team spirit. In the Japanese model, team spirit and teamwork are basic components in any organisation. Conflict and competition values are forbidden within Japanese organisations – but are encouraged with external societies.
3. The liberal model does not have the full commitment of workers at all levels for the achievement of organisational and societal objectives, because the objectives of workers may be different from those of the organisation. By contrast, the Japanese model is committed to satisfaction at both levels: the satisfaction of the organisation and the satisfaction of workers. That is why there is more commitment on the part of workers to achieving organisational objectives. Shin-Ichi and Whitehill (1984) compared commitment and correlation among workers, a phenomenon that does not exist in American organisations.
4. Organisational objectives in the West focus on increasing profit, which is called 'present season cultivation'. In Japan, organisational objectives are to build empires, which might be called 'future cultivation'. Thurow emphasised that Japanese organisations are working toward building empires when they build productive groups (Thurow, 1990).
5. The general philosophy in the USA is to increase consumption practices, while in Japan it is to increase saving and investment. This is very clear from the distribution of profits and bonuses, which in the USA is about 82 per cent, but in Japan does not exceed 30 per cent, the rest of profits being reinvested (Thurow, 1990).
6. The general philosophy of the Japanese model covers all levels of common objectives, so all Japanese organisations serve the community. It emphasises the ultimate value of the Japanese, to enable them be the major economic power in the world.
7. The American government does not interfere with individuals, based on the freedom rule 'Let him work, let him pass, and don't restrict him in any way' (Thurow, 1990). The Japanese model is contrary to the American model. In Japan, the state takes responsibility for national development.
8. American political philosophy is based on two pillars. The first is that of democracy, in order to create individually excellent leaders through the election process; and

the second is that of neutrality, without no interference with the private sector or individuals. In Japan, democracy is the major means of political representation, but the emperor comes to power by inheritance and is the main source of authority. So cultural homogeneity and unified community are based on political centralisation.

Figure 7.3 illustrates the difference between the American system and the Japanese TQM system.

In the next chapter we will consider the different management philosophies in detail.

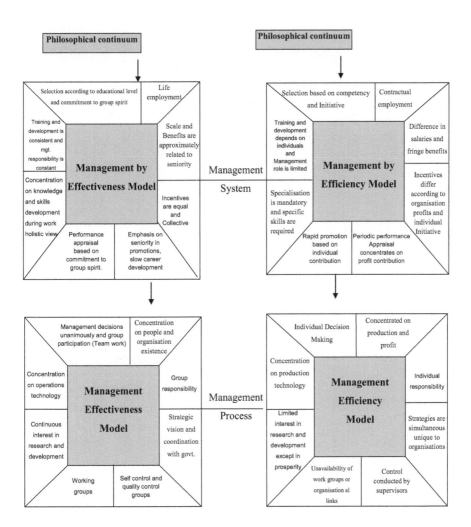

Figure 7.3   Liberal management model and Japanese management model

Note: Developed by Dr. Assaf, Team's Training Material of Total Quality management

8 I.Theory Systems

Introduction

THE PRIMACY OF VALUES

In Chapter 7, I presented a brief comparative overview of management philosophies, encompassing sufficiency, efficiency and effectiveness, but with no more than a hint at the Islamic context underlying the last of these three. In this chapter I present a more detailed comparison, based now on two assumptions: firstly, that our collective existence depends on the unification of individuals and groups, and secondly, that our individual and organisational values need to be aligned with those of society. Each management model has its own, societally based philosophy, and we shall see that this is also the case in the Arab and Islamic world. In my comparison I will focus on sufficiency, efficiency and effectiveness as illustrated, in theory if not also in practice, in the West, in Japan and in the Arab world (I.Theory). This comparison will then lead into the next chapter, in which I build up the components of I.Theory based on justice and other related values.

I will also indicate how different organisational processes apply in each philosophy/theory, such as those of leadership and decision making, performance management, planning and control processes. At the same time I will argue that the systems and corporate culture of I.Theory are the main factors involved, inclusive of approaches to learning, education and training to acquire knowledge, skills and attitudes.

A PHILOSOPHICAL TURNING-POINT

According to Jordanian management academic Assaf (2005),the so-called philosophy of 'management by effectiveness' was a turning-point, after the earlier management by efficiency and management by sufficiency, whereby and wherein:
The collective existence of any society is dependent on the level of unification between the individual and the group.

* The building up of civilisation depends on unification of societal and organisational levels. It is also dependent on the sets of values therein, whether they be those of the individual or of the group, political, economic or social. Assaf goes on to say: 'Justice is the core value for the establishment of any set of values leading to civilisation–happiness, in addition to the value of cooperation which represents the core work values for the group' (Assaf, 2005).

Before focusing on I.Theory as originally developed by Assaf, and which I have evolved further in my work with him, as we shall see later, we will first review in detail the Western and Japanese management philosophies and processes. In each case we will focus first on the philosophy in general, , and then on the implication both for human resources and for management and the organisation at large.

The Liberal Western Model: Sufficiency: Liberal 1

GENERAL ORIENTATION

Let us begin by saying that every management model has its own philosophy, which is necessary for the implementation and coordination of different processes among individuals, management and society at large, in its particular context. If there is any separation between individual, organisational and societal values contradictions will arise. If the management system meets with individual or collective resistance, changes will be required in order to realise a closer alignment between individuals, the organisation and society. I begin with what I term 'Liberal 1', the initial Western management model of 'sufficiency'.

THE PHILOSOPHY OF SUFFICIENCY

The 'Western' philosophy of sufficiency represented an important transition from the 'personal management' of a typical owner-entrepreneur to a new form of depersonalised management, distinguished by:

- A legal structure: law becomes highly significant for the organisation – applied to conduct with outside parties and to relationships between workers inside the organisation so that they do only what they are supposed to do.
- Scientific management: whereby principles, structures, and regulations control systems and management within the organisation.
- A depersonalised authority structure in the organisation: to influence planning and decision-making processes.
- Concentration of attention on economic sufficiency: to achieve the highest possible gain while ignoring social values that get in the way of this.
- Focusing on the physical/material environment inside the organisation that affects productivity, without taking any significant account of human factors.

We will now look at the implications for human resources management (HRM).

THE PHILOSOPHY OF SUFFICIENCY AND HUMAN RESOURCES MANAGEMENT

- Recruitment and selection is a contractual arrangement, based on specialised roles, efficiency requirements and performance capabilities, thereby selecting the right person for the right task.
- Work discipline is required so as to guarantee the literal application of all laws and regulations. The management consultant Emerson (Duncan, 1991) emphasised such discipline, specifically, and drew an analogy with a beehive. Frederick Taylor (Taylor, 1911) also affirmed the value of such a specialised work commitment.
- The organisation is hierarchical, with a vertical chain of command.

- Division of labour is absolute, backed by appropriate on-the-job training and pre-specified levels of productivity.
- It is assumed that employees seek only a material return.
- Precise performance records are kept. In this regard, Emerson (Duncan, 1991) says: 'It is not enough to depend on logical practices to feel satisfied about work progress, since documentation remains a must to go back to for building future plans.'

THE PHILOSOPHY OF SUFFICIENCY AND ORGANISATIONAL PROCESSES

We will now look at management and organisational 'sufficiency based' processes. A number of classical management philosophers, like the French industrial engineer Henri Fayol and Frederick Taylor, concentrated on the centrality of management processes in the organisation, especially those related to invariably top-down planning and decision-making processes, thereby involving:

1. Training: it is the responsibility of the organisation to train employees to handle and apply procedures and systems.
2. Systematisation and bureaucratisation: certifying employees' adherence to the law, circumscribing management interference except in the case of wrong-doing.
3. Performance appraisal: periodically, as a process of self-discipline.
4. Work study: for Taylor and Jaunt (Taylor, 1911) it was important to achieve a high degree of industrial efficiency; studying time and motion was one of the important techniques at this 'sufficiency' stage.

We will now consider 'efficiency'.

The Liberal Western Model: Efficiency: Liberal 2

GENERAL ORIENTATION

In America midway through the twentieth century there was a qualitative move in managerial thinking, away from 'scientific' and towards 'humanistic' management, towards, as it were, 'every employee a manager'. Productivity was now seen to be the result of teamwork and of intrinsic, as opposed to extrinsic, motivation. In the terms of this newly so-called 'human relations' theory, the human being was now seen to represent the most important factor in the production process and in the pursuit of efficiency.

HUMAN RESOURCES MANAGEMENT SYSTEMS AND THE EFFICIENCY ORIENTATION

The focus is now on both the person and the task, when choosing and recruiting, and on securing competitive advantage through human assets, whereby:

1. Promotions and incentive systems depend on initiatives by employees and the effects they have on employee performance.
2. The focus is on the division of labour as one requirement for achieving efficiency.

3. Training and development follow accordingly – to improve skills and capabilities.
4. Performance evaluation is based on fulfilling objectives (MBO).
5. Wage and salary differentials among employees are related to productivity levels.
6. There is an evaluation of non-material motives, such as empathy and recognition.

We now turn from human resources to the organisational system as a whole.

THE PHILOSOPHY OF EFFICIENCY AND THE ORGANISATIONAL SYSTEM

It was in fact at this time, from the 1960s onwards, initiated in America, that old-style, sufficiency-oriented 'personnel management', often linked with an enterprise's legal and administrative functioning, was separately identified as HRM:

- changing the view of the working person from that of a simple economic figure to that of a human being affected by the work environment
- changing perspectives on the management process and how rational it is, and focusing now, in particular, on the management of people, as well as tasks
- now viewing the organisation as an open world with close and continuous ties to its total internal and external environment.
- These changes dictate altogether new rules for the new, person-centred managerial order and the resulting philosophy of socio-technical efficiency.

We will now look at the Japanese-style, thereby comparing and contrasting these two 'Western' approaches with the prevailing 'Eastern' approach. It is important to stress that such an 'effective' Japanese management model prevailed in Japan, at least in the large manufacturing enterprises, from the 1960s to the 1980s, but by the 1990s and into the new millennium it had begun to wane as the Japanese miracle started to fade.

The Japanese and Islamic Approach to Effective Management

GENERAL ORIENTATION: COMPARING THE AMERICAN AND JAPANESE/ISLAMIC MODELS

It may be true to say that differences between management models relate to differences in the philosophy behind them. In fact, when we come to the intrinsic values of both liberal American and egalitarian Japanese models, we find that:

- The managerial philosophy behind the American model is based on rule-bound sufficiency and productivity-oriented efficiency values; whereas managerial philosophy in the Japanese model depends on effectiveness, in its broadest sense.
- From the Japanese perspective, the human factor (the human group) in the organisation is the primary constituent of effectiveness in the general sense of the word. Accordingly, the general manager of the Japanese electronics company Fujitsu said: 'We Japanese managers consider our employees to be [our] greatest assets. We treat them as treasures, and they respond with loyalty and hard work' (Takezawa and Whitehill, 1984).

- For Lester Thurow: 'The average turnover rate in American manufacturing is 4 percent per month. Almost 50 percent of the labour force of the typical American firms quits or is fired every twelve months' (Thurow, 1990) .Thurow also says: 'The Japanese with their emphasis on lifetime employment have very little turnover' (Thurow, 1990). He goes on to say: 'There is no way to build the climate of cooperation when dealing with a short-term employment system.'

Human Resource Management Systems

SELECTION AND RECRUITMENT

The process of recruitment and selection depends on criteria that range from the extreme Liberal model of America to the other extreme in Japan. The Liberal approach, on the one hand, depends on individual qualifications representing professional efficiency, regardless of value or societal aspects. The Japanese theory, on the other hand, depends on the social characteristics represented in the educational level and the level of commitment to the group spirit (Hammadi, 1988). In this, I.Theory is closer to the Japanese approach, as we shall see. It is based on two major elements:

1. *Strength*, which includes physical strength (mental, physical, psychological), scientific strength (credentials and specialisation) and professional skills and experience. This means that strength is here more profound and thorough – certainly more than physical strength – than it is presented as being in other theories.
2. *Honesty*, in the general sense of the word, which relates to people's entitlements (both material and non-material, transferable and fixed) with which a human being can be trusted. The professional connotation of 'honesty' is in the nature of the assignments and goals of the job becoming trustworthy, in that they must be delivered requisitely to whomever it may concern, the 'whom' in this case being the owners of the organisation and the shareholders, whether the organisation is private or public.

Islamic lore has affirmed those two factors more than once in the holy Qur'an. Allah says in *sura* Al-Qasas (The Narration), *aya* 26: '*Surely the best man to employ is one who is strong and honest.*'

THE EMPLOYMENT CONTRACT

What is the difference between the contractual appointment and permanent employment? In general terms, the contract is signed between the employee and the employer; whereas in reality, the contract is set between three separate interests: the organisation's interests, the employee's interests and society's interests. We must ensure that these interests are, first and foremost, in agreement with the effectiveness conditions as a high-level value. This point should be taken into consideration at the beginning of the employment action. None of these three interests should have priority over the other.

The Liberal approach chooses the contractual employment style in accordance with the value of liberty, which, when applied, gives every party the right to abandon the other party when it feels it necessary to do so. It also accords with the value of competition, which enables employers to choose the most efficient among job seekers, and permits them to dismiss the less efficient the minute they want to do so.

In the Japanese model, however, permanent employment is sought so as to give workers a chance to feel safe, in accordance with the philosophy of co-operation, which is considered the highest value in the area of employment. The organisation cannot address problems by letting go of the least useful and most harmful employees, because they are protected by permanent employment contracts.

PROMOTION

There are two bases for promotion in I.Theory:

- *Faith*: This value is considered the final arbiter for the set of values. It is relevant for all persons, according to their particular faith, to a degree determined by the will of the person him- or herself. Here, faith and commitment do not have to be directly tied to a particular job or post. Thus, the basis of faith becomes the safety valve for public responsibility.
- *Knowledge*: This is the second basis for promotion, and represents, with faith, the duality of faith–knowledge, with more concentration on knowledge as a criterion for elevation inside the group, including that those in charge should be provided with the laws and regulations needed to manage group affairs.

WAGES AND SALARIES

The justice value requires the setting of wages and salaries based on the following criteria:

- Fairness: by paying an equal wage for equal work of equal employment status. What threaten most organisations are large disparities in salary for positions of equal rank, and indeed between ranks. This is abundantly evident in the Liberal model.
- Not having great variations in the salary scale. This prevents ill-will or struggles between management and labour within the same enterprise, also preventing social inequality.
- Conforming to the minimum wage and meeting the minimum requirements for a basic standard of living, accompanied by a fair pay-raise system that takes into account inflation and variations in the standard of living.

TYPES OF INCENTIVE

Incentives are important for motivating employees, deepening their commitment to group goals and urging them to work to achieve those goals.

The most important constituent of a motivational system, according to I.Theory, is the focus on satisfaction and not fulfilment, since satisfaction resides in the inner self, whereas fulfilment resides in desires. The inner self is easily satisfied (especially if one has faith), whereas desire cannot be satisfied except for short periods of time.

ORGANISATIONAL PROCESSES

Organisational processes include the following:

Leadership and decision-making process: Firstly, according to I.Theory, the overarching value is that of justice; thus, the responsibility of leadership in any society is to enhance the promotion of this primary value, as well as the secondary values that go along with it. The effectiveness value in I.Theory requires the leader to 'manage by detached involvement'. That means that he or she will not side with one party against another within the group. Moreover, the leader should perform the strategic planning for the group in order to be able to identify the options that fulfil the goals represented by the civilisation–well-being duality.

Moreover, I.Theory requires that the leader should be careful to combine the different aspects of authority, such as:

- Authority as a *right*, which represents the official dimension in the leader.
- Authority as *power*, which represents real depth in the leader's personality.
- Authority as *capability*, which represents the professional dimension in the leader's personality.

Performance and managerial processes in the organisation, secondly, rest on the efficiency of productivity, which aims to accomplish the highest possible productivity at the lowest possible cost, in the shortest possible time and with the highest quality. Combined, these factors lead to enhanced profits. They also focus on the human being in the organisation, who is required to support the organisation (its permanency and progress), based on unification between three basic factors:

- enhancing the profits to be distributed to shareholders
- enhancing material and non-material gains to employees and society
- enhancing the possibility of improvements and continued development for the organisation.

Defining responsibility in the workplace: The assumption, thirdly, is that planning will be everybody's task; it is never the responsibility of some rather than others.

The planning process, fourthly, is done according to the following:

- Unifying the duality of present and future in a way that helps to deal with current circumstances while focusing on immediate goals. In this case, there is a focus on long-term top goals, including the ways and means of securing the accomplishment of goals. Most important is making the connection between the present and the future in a way that focuses on present goals without hindering the successful completion of future goals, and vice versa. This planning must be done, first and foremost, for the purpose of unifying the two sides of this duality.
- Unifying the whole–part duality during the planning process means that a comprehensive view should be built into the strategic planning process, spanning all processes and variables.

Control processes, fifthly, are based on the quality of unification, that is, between internal self-control and external social control, namely, the unofficial and the official. Internal self-control rests on the set of individual values, those of life, represented in the value of holiness. It is not possible to be sure of the existence of control in any organisation unless it is established on values of this sort – values that define the individual's relationship with him- or herself. As for social control, it is more of a supporting process for internal control. Whenever individual self-awareness and control diminishes, and whatever the factors that slow down the self-motivating power of the person, this social control helps to create an atmosphere of external order in the shape of group awareness.

Research and development: Sixthly, scientific research, for me both social (including I.Theory) and natural, is the key to development, and development is the key to a better future. Early on, the Japanese realised the significance of this, both socially and technically, and gave it due attention. This included assigning it a significant budget and distinguished leadership, together with a specified mission for research, learning and development as a top priority within each organisation.

Technological processes: Finally, there should be a dual, unified focus on processes and technologies, again in both a social and a technical sense, taking into consideration both production technology and the building of a series of relationships that guarantee the inclusion and development of the technology, both physically and people-wise, to be used in serving productive and social processes.

We now turn more generally to the effectiveness philosophy in the management of organisations.

Organisational Management

Whereas in the 'Western', American model the organisation, more especially in the 'sufficiency' case, is treated as a machine, in the 'Eastern', Japanese case, until the 1990s at least, it was treated much more like a human organism. That having been said, the 'human relations' school of management in America, from the 1950s onwards, was much more organic in orientation that its 'scientific management' predecessors. However, from the 1990s onwards this movement seems to have been subverted by the onset of 'shareholder capitalism' in the post-Reagan and post-Thatcher era.

Ironically, and at the same time, in the 1990s the Japanese bubble began to burst, the by now famous 'art of Japanese management' came unstuck, and in the new millennium we had, seemingly, nowhere to turn for an overall, effective – in both the socio-cultural and the techno-economic sense – approach to management.

Conclusion

My own work on I.Theory, as a further development of that undertaken by Dr Assaf, takes up, in a sense, from where these 'Western' and 'Eastern' models have left off. While the approach to human as well as technical and economic 'efficiency' (Liberal 2), so to speak, was indeed a 'Western' step forward, from a humanistic perspective, there seems to have been a regression in more recent times, from the 1990s onwards. Though companies in America and Europe talk of 'people as our greatest asset', the bottom line seems to have reasserted itself with a vengeance.

In the Japanese 'East', a similar human regression has occurred over the past two decades, for two reasons. Firstly, from the 1990s onwards, as the macro-economy became increasingly overrun by speculation in the wake of Japan's failure to develop its own, effective overall economic orientation, so the demise of the Japanese miracle inhibited managerial effectiveness. Secondly, and almost at the same time, the rise and rise of Japan's historic rival, China, heightened Japan's inferiority complex vis–à–vis its all-powerful neighbour. The tragic earthquake and tsunami of 2011 have not helped in this respect.

Figures 8.1 and 8.2 summarise the key features of the model of HRM based on I. Theory, as elaborated above.

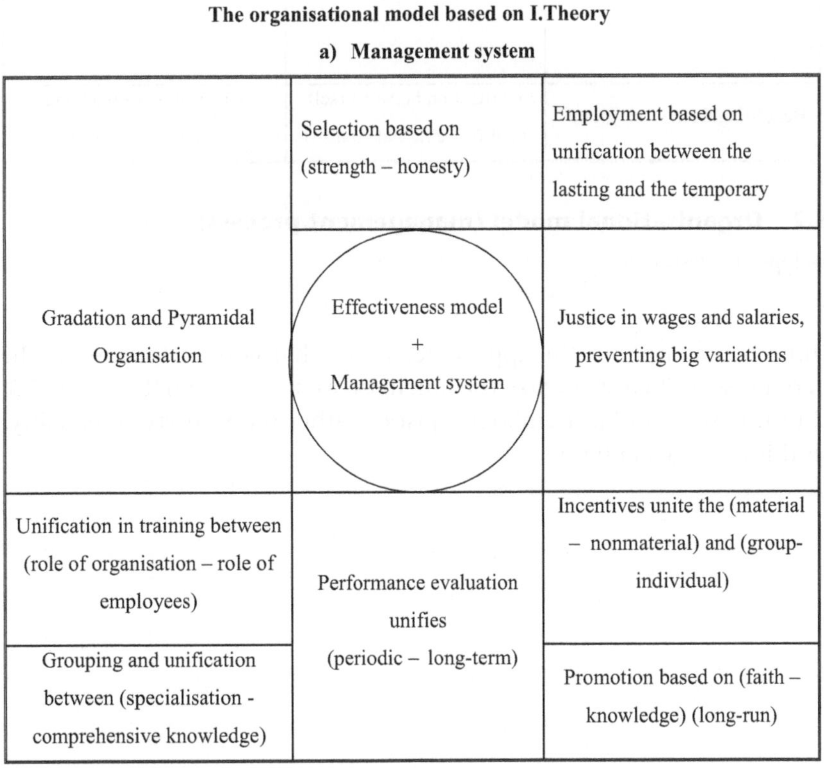

The organisational model based on I.Theory

a) Management system

	Selection based on (strength – honesty)	Employment based on unification between the lasting and the temporary
Gradation and Pyramidal Organisation	Effectiveness model + Management system	Justice in wages and salaries, preventing big variations
Unification in training between (role of organisation – role of employees)	Performance evaluation unifies (periodic – long-term)	Incentives unite the (material – nonmaterial) and (group-individual)
Grouping and unification between (specialisation - comprehensive knowledge)		Promotion based on (faith – knowledge) (long-run)

Figure 8.1   The organisational model (management system)

Source: Assaf, A. 'I.Theory for Excellence'. 2005, p. 421

a) **The Management Process**

Unification between (process – production) technology	Unification and grouping between (group - individual style) in the decision making process	Unification between (profit - employees – society)
Significance of scientific research	Effectiveness model + Management Process	Systematic unification between responsibilities of (individual – group)
Benefiting from work groups	Unification between (self control – external control)	Unification of planning (present – future)

Figure 8.2   Organisational model (management process)

Source: Developed by Researcher

The time is now ripe for the appearance of an alternative – for the Middle Eastern model, in our case 'I.Theory', to take the limelight, as it were, from 'East' and 'West'. Born and bred in the Arab world, it embodies justice rather than liberty or equality. We will now flesh this out in Chapter 9.

9 *The Values of I.Theory*

Introduction

THE TIME IS RIPE FOR EVOLUTION IN MANAGEMENT

We now come to the cornerstone of this book, at least from a theoretical perspective, before addressing its application in two case studies. At a time when, as we saw in the last chapter, both 'Western' and 'Eastern' management models are failing to fulfil their earlier promise, the time is ripe for an evolution. From my Arab perspective, that is 'I.Theory'. A further reason why such a new management theory is called for is that neither of the two rising economic powers, China and India, is coming up with a new, fully fledged management model. Moreover, management-wise, the continent of Europe, has always been eclipsed by America.

MANAGEMENT BY VALUES

This chapter covers the integrated value system in Islam that supports 'I. (Islamic) Theory/Management by Values' (Assaf, 2005). This value system leads to the creation of an environment for a culturally oriented approach to management. Whereas the West focuses on individual freedom and the Japanese 'East' on social equality, we take Islamic justice as the core management value: political, social and economic.

HOW CAN WE CREATE A MANAGEMENT THEORY BASED ON OUR CULTURE?

Since 2003, Jordanian management academic Dr Assaf has been working with me at TEAM Jordan, as a senior management consultant. During one of our meetings I raised a question: How can we create a management theory to implement inside our organisations that is based on our culture, instead of Western or Eastern management theories, and thereby become pioneers in our work as management consultants?

Dr Assaf said there and then that he had already begun work on an Islamic theory of management, based on Islamic thought and values. He explained the main ideas of his theory. Generally, I agreed, and asked him if we could make a start by applying it through our consultancy company, as well as through my doctoral work. I asked whether it meant that we had to change all our organisational systems accordingly. He replied, 'Yes, indeed.'

I felt strongly, as I always have, that we had to build a new culture, based first of all on values and ethics. For me, ethics and values are the most important elements in building good organisations and good societies.

Six months later, TEAM won a bid for organisational development. It was for a computer programming company owned by the Jordanian Islamic Organisation. I said that it was a great opportunity to implement our new management theory (Islamic Theory). In the first meeting with the senior management team we presented the different approaches to organisational development, including Western theories and the Japanese (TQM) theory, and informed the team about the Liberal (L) model, in which freedom plays a role in society and organisations and which considers the impact of effectiveness mainly in terms of conflict and competition, and not on the basis of unity as a crucial value.

The management team agreed that we could begin our experimentation with I.Theory with its company.

Freedom, Equality and Justice

ISLAM: THE CULMINATING 'BOOK' RELIGION

The basic value of 'I.Theory' is 'justice' Assaf (2005). According to Assaf, this is the ultimate core value for any society or organisation, or for life as a whole. For me, this notion comes across very clearly in monotheistic religious thought. The three 'book' religions came from the same source, so between them the emphasis on justice is not very different. Justice is the ultimate core value in all respects, and the remaining values follow; and Islam was the culminating 'book' religion. It explained and clarified this concept as a core value for all believers. Allah said in *sura* al-Baqara (The Cow), *aya* 285: '*The prophet believes in what has been revealed to him by his lord, and so do the faithful, each one believes in God and his angels, His books and the prophets and we make no distinction between the apostles.*'

We shall now see how Islamic theory depends on the two major issues of equality and justice.

FREEDOM, EQUALITY AND JUSTICE COMPARED AND CONTRASTED

Justice, equality and freedom: in spite of the differences between authors and philosophers in their interpretation of these values, what is the meaning of each one? Which one of the three is the ultimate core value?

Justice

Justice is based on the following elements:

- It is a *collective* value based on a group of people and their interrelationship, and the ambiguity in their relationships, as well as on the need to confront ambiguity.
- It is a human value that seeks the *truth*.
- It is a *practical* value in the life of groups, aimed at maintaining balance in the community.
- It must be a *normative* value with social, political, economic and judicial authority.
- It must be applied by the governing *authority*, which is committed to it.

Thus, the concept of justice might be defined as follows: It is a moral value inherent in the consciousness of human groups, covering group relationships, defending development, without any feeling of oppression.

Equality

The following are the main elements pertaining to equality:

- When there are differences among individuals within a group, the need to implement equality increases. This means that there is *no discrimination* on the basis of colour, nationality or race.
- There are differences between justice and equality in that equality has more of a *legal* than a *moral* value.
- Equality is a *contradictory* value in itself. Conceptually, it considers all people equal; but in reality, competition creates differences between individuals.
- Equality comprises some negative aspects. It *may limit innovation* in those who excel, and encourage passivism in others.

Freedom

The chief elements of freedom are:

- It is a human and *individual value*, but not a group value. Therefore, the freedom of the group is an individual freedom.
- Keeping a *balance* between individual freedom and group, or indeed communal, affiliation and responsibility, is thereby *problematic*.
- Freedom is a total, *unified value*, and cannot be considered separately in terms of social freedom, political freedom or economic freedom.
- Authority has the power to abolish the freedom of individuals or groups. Thus, this value is *aligned with struggle*.

If any group has an identity, it must have one ultimate core value. So which value is the ultimate core value? At the individual level, there is no doubt that freedom is the ultimate core value, but at the human group level, justice is the core. Let us now explore how it manifests itself politically, socially and economically.

Political, Social and Economic Justice

JUSTICE AS A POLITICAL VALUE SYSTEM

These values are related to political authority as the basis of any human group's existence, whatever its level or size. The unity of authority is the embodiment of the unity of the group and its sustainability. The only value that guarantees this unification and sustainability, from an Islamic perspective, is the justice value. So the main role of political authority is to maintain unified group security so as to achieve the objective – happiness/well-being. Authority cannot achieve the objective without the important value related to justice.

Sovereignty must come from the inner group, self-correlated with its will. The will value is capable of transformation and structure, and of achieving the ultimate core value.

There are many values correlated with the will value, such as:

- A safety and security value: only the authority that has the will can implement safety and security for all individuals and groups.
- A development value, based on achieving sustained group power.
- A welfare value, based on the individual's realisation of happiness.

The sub-values of sovereignty, security, development and welfare are related to the state or, in our case, enterprise, with its ultimate core value: justice. Whenever implementation depends on a business organisation, the development value is replaced by the organisation's social role and the welfare value is replaced by the workers' objectives. The standard measure is the ultimate goal (civilisation–happiness) and justice is the ultimate core value.

JUSTICE AS A SOCIAL VALUE SYSTEM

Justice pertains to any society or social entity, based on its unification and balance. To achieve the unification of individual/group, there must be no contradiction between them and their attempt to achieve harmony. In order to build a social system, it is a must to profess a pure social value system based on healthy social relationships between people. Allah says in *sura* Al-Hujurat (The Private Apartments), *aya* 13: '*O humankind, we created you from a male and female, and we made you races and tribes for you to get to know each other. The most noble of you in the sight of God are those of you who are most conscientious. And God is omniscient, fully aware.*'

Also *aya* 10 of the same *sura*: '*The faithful are surely brothers.*'

On the other hand, there are other related values, such as solidarity and cordiality. Allah says in *sura* Al-Roum (The Romans), *aya* 21: '*creating love and compassion between you*'.

JUSTICE AS AN ECONOMIC VALUE SYSTEM

Justice is related to the economic system to the extent that it organises and unifies it. Thus the relationship between the state and the individual, via the public sector and the private sector, is all important. In addition to the justice value as an ultimate core value, there is an economic equilibrium value to sustain all the economic relationships in an integrated, unifying system. From this economic equilibrium, there follow three major economic values:

1. *Saving value*: Islamic doctrine differentiates between saving and hoarding. Hoarding is forbidden, because it will keep wealth within a small group of people, which leads to an unbalanced economy. Allah says in *sura* At-Tawba (The Repentance), *ayas* 34 and 35: '*Believers, many priests and monks consume the wealth of the people in vain, and hinder them from the way of God. And there are those who hoard gold and silver and do not spend it on the way of God. So inform them of the painful punishment, on a day when the fire of hell will rage against that, and their foreheads and sides and backs will be seared*

by it. This is what you hoarded for yourselves, so enjoy what you have been hoarding!' In modern societies, especially in underdeveloped societies, to hoard is dangerous, because accumulating wealth in any society and saving it in foreign banks means damaging one society in the interests of another.

2.   *Investment value*: This value is the basis of economic development and creating the combined development of agricultural and industrial sectors, on the one hand, and basic services, on the other. Capital expenditure is an important investment because it is based on unification between individuals and groups to increase the wealth of individuals and develop society.

3.   *Consumption value*: This is the tributary of the investment process. It aims at achieving balance between investment and consumption. It also aims to achieve individual welfare, based on a balance between basic needs and ultimate needs. Allah says in *sura* Al-Isra (The Night of Journey), *aya* 29: *'And don't keep your hand bound to your neck, nor yet stretch it as far as it extends, lest you become reprehensible and destitute.'* He also said in *sura* Al-Furqan (The Criterion), *aya* 67: *'And those who, when they spend, are neither extravagant nor stingy, but right in between.'*

We now turn to the work value, in the context of justice.

Justice and Work Values

FROM ECONOMIC EFFICIENCY TO SOCIO-ECONOMIC EFFECTIVENESS

Justice-oriented values have a unifying effect within the organisation. They are related to socio-economic effectiveness as an ultimate core value in the business organisation. In contrast, a competitive or conflict-laden value is the core value in the Liberal model and in all organisations that base their work on the freedom value. The Japanese model concentrates on the co-operation value as a core value to unify all the objectives in the organisation. In fact, I.Theory concentrates on this value too, but it is not based on teamwork or social equality in work in the same way as in the Japanese model. The key value is justice because it guarantees the unification of teamwork and individual work, and the organisation's soul and the individual's soul, in order to link organisational objectives with individual objectives so as to achieve civilisation and happiness.

FOCUSING ON CO-OPERATION

Such a unifying value is very clear in the holy Qur'an; the emphasis is on positive, and not negative, co-operation. Allah says in the *sura* Al-Maeda (the Feast), *aya* 2: *'Help each other to kindness and conscience, and do not help each other to crime and animosity. For God is severe with consequences.'* Also in Islam, there is no call to competition, except for limited appeals that are linked to believers' good deeds. Allah says in *sura* Al-Mutafifin (The Cheaters), *aya* 26: *'The seal thereof will be musk: and for this let those aspire, who have aspirations.'* This competition will never threaten the group or lead to conflict between believers in the same society, because that would contradict the unified values that bring together all groups' energies and efforts for the achievement of the ultimate core value.

In this focus on the co-operation value, there are some ten related sub-values:

1. *Obligations value*: This value in the Islamic faith is not coercive; rather, it is defined by doctrinal regulations that aim to organise the lives of people and to help them achieve their real objectives. This value is different from the obligations value in the Liberal model in the West, which is based on fear of authority to achieve the authority's interest. It also coincides with the co-operation value, strengthening relations between individuals and groups.

2. *Acceptance and satisfaction value*: This value is based on the human inner self and is harmonised with the general or special objectives of individuals and groups. The Japanese perceived the importance of this value as the basis for achieving co-operation and acceptance within the group in order to achieve unification between the objectives of the individual and those of the group. This value is mentioned in *sura* At-Tawba (The Repentance), *aya* 59: *'If only they had been content with what God and God's messenger gave them, and said, "God is sufficient for us; God! God and the messenger of God will give to us of the bounty of God: It is to God that we make our request."'*

3. *Obedience value*: This value unifies obligation with acceptance, authority with the group, and the relationship between the group and the individual. The stipulation is that orders that have to be obeyed should be correct and in accordance with Allah's, for otherwise man cannot obey them because 'No creature is obedient if he is disobedient to the Creator [Allah].' This idea is reiterated in *sura* Al-Insan (The Human), *aya* 24: *'So be constant to the wisdom of your Lord, and don't be obedient to the sinner or the atheist among them.'* Obedience implies enthusiasm and initiative in implementation; whereas with the acceptance value, the request is only implemented without any conditions of enthusiasm or initiative.

4. *Discipline value*: This value is linked with obligation, which implies respect for laws and regulations, in addition to instructions and procedures, in order to guarantee that work is undertaken that is for a purpose.

5. *Commitment value*: This value is linked with both the satisfaction and obedience values and is rooted in the mind and soul. The value lends power and energy to the group in its endeavour to achieve goals.

6. *Perfection value*: This value is mainly linked with commitment, rooted in the inner self and group soul. This is very clear in *aya* 30 of *sura* Al-Kahf (The Cave): *'We will not neglect the reward of any who does even one good deed.'* The Prophet also said: *'Allah loves to see one's job done at the level of itqan.'*

7. *Loyalty value*: This value is related to the vertical relationship between the authority and the individuals within the group, organisation, family and state. But this loyalty is not a blind one, it must be a conscious loyalty, with the condition that the authority of justice obtains individual loyalty.

8. *Integration value*: This value relates to the feeling of individuals as a part of the group; each must accept the others with satisfaction and respect.

9. *Selflessness and sacrifice value*: Selflessness is related to the loyalty value and to preferring the interest of the group over individual interests. Sacrifice is related to merging with others and is linked with Islamic doctrine, especially with *Jihad* (holy war). Allah says in *sura* At-Tawba (The Repentance), *aya* 20: *'Those who believe, and go into exile and struggle in the cause of God with their possessions and their persons are greater in rank in the sight of God; and they are the ones who attain salvation.'*

10. *Individual value system (life values)*: The individual is the basic unit in human existence; therefore, the personality of the individual and his or her life must be consistent with life values in order to attain happiness. It also needs to be consistent with the organisation's structure and its sustainability and development.

These individual values are the core values of total group values.

Conclusion

ETERNAL VALUES: TAQWA AND TAWHEED

In the final analysis, the Liberal model emphasises the 'initiative' value, which is based on freedom as a life value. The Japanese model emphasises the 'commitment' value, which is based on social equality as a life value. I.Theory is different from the other models because the individual values are not established as life values only. Allah linked and organised individual values with the eternity value (life–afterlife) and now–future. Allah says in *sura* Al-Qasas (The Narration), *aya* 77: '*But seek the abode of the hereafter with what God has bestowed on you, and do not forget your part in this world. And be good as God has been good to you. And do not seek corruption on earth, for God does not love the corrupt.*'

In Islam, the value of worship is the core of people's lives . Allah says in *aya* 56 of *sura* Ath-Thariyat (The Scattering Winds): '*And I only created sprites and humans, for them to serve Me.*' The core value here is the piety value (*taqwa*), because real piety is not only implemented through religious ritual; it is the fear of Allah in the inner self, inside the organisation and inside society. The faith value, as a positive result of the two values mentioned above, is an internal dialogue between mind and self. The three integrated values emphasise the real religious personality, which is based on *tawheed*.

To enhance the piety value, there are other values linked with it, such as kindness, awe and charity values. There are other values linked to and integrated with the above values, such as the straightforwardness value, based on human mental powers; the asceticism value, based on self and linked to the straightforwardness value; and the sincerity value, which means sincerity towards God in all sayings and works.

As for piety, there are other value systems, such as truth, based on the inner self; trust in everything: God, humans, work and so on; and devotion, which is linked to trust. This value is not related only to materialistic issues, but covers all rights or duties of all moral or materialistic values related to the human being and his relationship with God, himself or others. Many *aya*s emphasise all previous values, which shows that these individual values are rooted in doctrinal systems within the Islamic system.

THE VALUE OF PIETY AND FAITH

There are other values related to the worship value and integrated with the piety value, such as:

* *Glorification value*, which is the basic value in the worship value and covers all kinds of obedience to God and fulfilling all duties.

- *Reflection value*, which means reflecting about the Creator (God) and the rules of the universe. This value covers all the insights and the components of the universe.
- *Gratitude value*, which is the mental appreciation of and self-aspiration to what the human being has achieved in his thought and glory. Man accepts and appreciates the gift granted to us by God, so he has to thank God.

The Faith value is linked with other value systems, such as:

- *Grandness value*: To appreciate the Almighty and His characteristics, all that he granted humankind, and all life rules and regulations.
- *Trust in God*: To believe that man's soul belongs to God, and that God is omnipotent. This value is also related to the future; but this reliance does not cancel out the importance of the human being's work using his own knowledge, but instead gives him or her the power to feel depressed if he or she fails to achieve the desired outcomes.
- *Submission value*: This is linked with the reliance value, but there is a difference between them: the reliance value is associated with the beginning of the work, while the submission value is associated with the completion of the work and the acceptance of outcomes. This matter represents real goodness and keeps the balance of character in human nature.
- *Patience value:* This value might be considered an indicator of the submission value. It keeps balance in the personality of the human being, even if he is in difficult circumstances.

If people implement all these values in their life and work, and feel that their efforts are rewarded, they will be encouraged to do everything with quality. Ultimately, this will be reflected in all aspects of life and people will be closer to reaching satisfaction and happiness.

MY ROLE IN IMPLEMENTING I.THEORY

My role in the last few years has been to create an awareness campaign in the Arab world by implementing our values and the core value: justice. As an integral management consultant, I focus on values in all my work assignments – at least during the past three years. So when I implement any standards, I use all the concepts of I.Theory, as rooted in our culture and religion.

Figures 9.1 and 9.2 present a summary of I.Theory values and demonstrate the total unification values system:

I will now present the case studies of RSCN and Al-Quds Paints Co., to demonstrate the effect of the implementation of different components of I.Theory, based on the co-operative inquiry methodology.

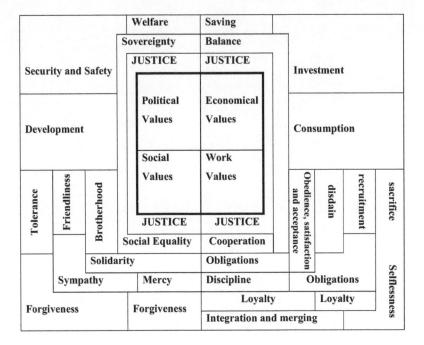

Figure 9.1   Total unified value system

Source: Assaf, 2005, *I Theory*, p. 303

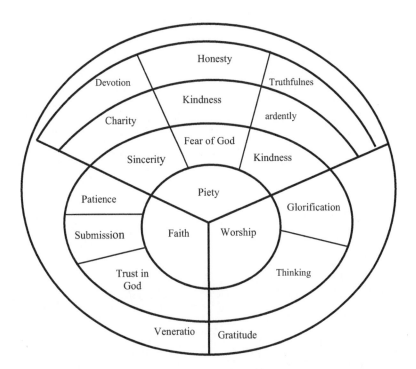

Figure 9.2   Life value system from an Islamic perspective

Source: Assaf, 2005, *I Theory*, p. 303

10 *Case Study 1: Royal Society for the Conservation of Nature, Amman*

Introduction

INTRODUCING CO-OPERATIVE INQUIRY

Having described the context of my work and society, the methodology I will be adopting, and the theory that underlies it, I now come to the application of I.Theory. To me as a consultant and an agent of transformation operating in the Islamic and Arab world, these two case applications are crucial. I start with RSCN.

The story that I tell here of the application of I.Theory in RSCN explores the role that management by values/I.Theory plays in charting a transformation path, which RSCN is seeking to achieve. Drawing on John Heron's *Co-operative Inquiry* (Heron, 1996) and Robert Yin's (2003) case-study method, I draw, in particular, on culture and nature. The case application was supported by RSCN Director General Yehya Khaled, who had already gone through the transformation journey during his two years of study at the University of Buckingham, together with his RSCN co-researchers. All of us strove to develop TQM based on indigenous culture and Islamic concepts. RSCN is highly committed to values, ethics and its mission to serve and protect the Jordanian community.

THE AGENDA WE WERE ADDRESSING

The agenda we were addressing together in our co-operative inquiry was:

1. How can we develop a management theory based on our Islamic values that leads to enhanced quality and transformation?
2. What is the role of I.Theory in supporting the development of quality management and transformation at RSCN?

Let me now introduce you to, first, RSCN and, second, the co-operative inquirers.

THE ROYAL SOCIETY FOR THE CONSERVATION OF NATURE

For 40 years, RSCN has devoted itself to saving life. It began by saving the life of endangered species, like the magnificent Arabian oryx, which was about to disappear from Jordan. It then devoted much of its energy to saving the life of whole areas, like Dana, Mujib and Azraq, with a view to protecting Jordan's most beautiful wild places. It also invested in the lives of young Jordanians through its school and student programmes, which help future generations to value their natural heritage.

RSCN is a non-governmental organisation that was created in 1966 under the patronage of King Hussein. It is devoted to the protection of nature through the instruments of sustainable development (RSCN Report, 2005)

During the 1970s, the government of Jordan made RSCN responsible for establishing and managing nature reserves and enforcing wildlife protection laws. It has also been very active in environmental research and education. Among its achievements are:

1. The establishment of seven nature reserves.
2. The successful conservation of endangered species, including the Arabian oryx.
3. The creation of over 1,000 nature conservation clubs in Jordanian schools, helping students to understand environmental issues.
4. The creation of a national database on habitats and species.
5. The regulation of illegal hunting throughout the kingdom.
6. The development of large-scale conservation projects designed to integrate environmental protection with the socio-economic development of local people. (RSCN Report, 2004)

RSCN currently has about 280 permanent staff within four functional divisions: Conservation, Outreach, Wild Jordan, and Administration and Finance. (RSCN/Human Resources Department)

THE CAST OF CO-RESEARCHERS

The following are brief profiles of the members of the co-operative inquiry team.

- *Yehya Khaled: Director General of RSCN*: Born in 1972 to a Palestinian refugee family, who used to live in a poor area in Amman. He studied in United Nations Relief and Works Agency schools and left an indelible mark in every school he attended. In 1994, he received his bachelor's degree in Applied Biology from Jordan University for Science and Technology. He started work at RSCN as an interim researcher, and then became a full-time section head at the age of 23. In 1997, he became a qualified regional trainer in different fields, among which were reserves management, management training and institutional development. Yehya then developed the RSCN charter in order to establish a values system; in addition, he endeavoured to move RSCN from a local to a global vision, building on local culture and nature. Thereafter he looked for a team to help him in the process of organisational transformation. The team included the following members:
- *Rami Jihad: Regional Training Manager*: Joined RSCN in February 2004. He previously worked with international companies in Saudi Arabia, such as General Motors,

which exposed him to indigenous Islamic and Arab culture alongside an exogenous, American-style multinational. Rami is involved in learning and development, which normally requires him to identify and respond to people in need of development. In the process, he has sought opportunities to incorporate the value of justice into the organisation and to reflect it in all of RSCN's activities, especially in the human resources department.

- *Nash'at Hamidan: Conservation Specialist*: Is a Technical Adviser for the protected areas, and Manager and Central Ecologist at RSCN. His major field of expertise is in the development and implementation of management plans for Jordan's network of protected areas; planning and implementation of research and monitoring programmes for Jordan's wildlife within and outside protected areas; reporting, team planning and capacity building for Jordan's protected areas; management planning, wildlife research and monitoring, GIS and digital mapping systems. Nash'at's involvement at RSCN is therefore both strategic and technical.
- *Enas Sakkijha: Research and Survey Section Head*: Is responsible for a team of 11 members. She focuses on building team spirit and transferring knowledge to new staff; in addition, she is a technical specialist in flora, fauna and GIS. Her involvement in the transformation process is very clear, starting with capacity building in the research team, strengthening team spirit and transferring knowledge to new staff.
- *Mohammad Qawaba': Manager of Dana Nature Reserve*, which aims to conserve biodiversity and natural habitats over an area of 300 km² and its surroundings in an integrated way, focused on socio-economic aspects and public awareness. Mohammad is also a graduate of the Transformation Management programme. He holds a degree in mechanical engineering and has a keen interest in nature. He has developed a unique approach to transforming and re-establishing Dana Reserve as a place for human growth and knowledge creation.
- *Raja' Tubah: Administration Section Head*: Supervises, develops and manages all administrative and personnel aspects at RSCN, in accordance with its strategic plan and objectives. In addition, she manages, develops and conducts capacity building for the Administration and Human Resource team to ensure effective support for all RSCN's operations and transformation. She helped Yehya to build an HR system, taking into account her long experience at RSCN. The fruit of her hard work with the senior management on this issue is that a new salary scale is being developed at RSCN through a process of transformation based on the justice value.

Initiating the Co-operative Inquiry

FIRST REFLECTION PHASE

During the initial two meetings with the co-operative inquiry team at RSCN, and after they had attended two workshops on the subject given by Dr Assaf, I discussed the concepts of I.Theory. I explained the difference between management by sufficiency, efficiency and effectiveness, and how we can identify the major issues related to each management style: Western, Japanese and Islamic. I also explained what set I.Theory apart: firstly, how we can strike a balance of emphasis between the individual and the group; secondly, how we can ensure continual improvement; thirdly, how we should best incorporate Islamic values.

FIRST ACTION PHASE

Participation and knowledge creation

In the first six months of 2006 a plan of action was launched for the first action phase, to explore I.Theory and the concept of a values-managed organisation. Some co-operative inquiry team members agreed, while others did not because they felt that they needed more time to understand it and create an enabling culture for acceptance of the theory. This reflected Heron's idea of democratic participation and reflection, which in fact also embodied *Shura* (consultation).

During each co-operative inquiry meeting we discussed one or more of the stages of the modes of co-operative inquiry: for instance, co-researchers' *experiential* knowledge and how they should use and reflect it to RSCN's benefit; and their *imaginal* knowledge and how they might use it to enhance their planning skills. In what follows, I will go over my discussions with the co-operative researchers and explore how they each embodied the conceptual knowledge of quality management or built an organisational value system based on the core value of I.Theory.

Knowledge modes and the I.Theory concept

During our meetings, we got the idea that there was not enough understanding of the concept of I.Theory, except that it meant a kind of change and that leadership needed to be encouraged to make it happen. During our workshops we developed a questionnaire (Appendix 1) based on the four epistemic modes of co-operative inquiry:

- Experiential knowledge: evident in meeting and feeling the presence of some energy, entity, person, place, process or thing.
- Imaginal knowledge: evident in the institutive grasp of the significance of patterns expressed in graphic, musical, or verbal art forms.
- Propositional knowledge: conceptually and linguistically based.
- Practical knowledge: evident in exercising skill.

In that multifaceted knowledge context, we addressed these questions:

1. How can we develop a management theory based on our Islamic values that leads to enhanced quality and transformation?
2. What is the role of I.Theory in supporting the development of quality management and transformation?

I explained: 'I.Theory is based on a number of principles, which include the need to build human organisations, socially, politically as well as commercially. These organisations will be comprised of many elements, the most important of which should be the human being. Related to that will be a values system forming the moral basis for the organisation, and we should build human resource systems accordingly.'

SECOND REFLECTION PHASE: REFLECTING ON THE JUSTICE VALUE

Justice is relative and not easy to measure

In April 2006 I presented the justice value for discussion by all the co-operative inquiry team with a view to its implementation at RSCN. The way I saw it, justice was the most important value and the core value in business. *Taqwa* (God-fearing behaviour) is the core value in our lives in the Arab world, just as equality and freedom are important in the Japanese and American cases. Justice does not preclude freedom or equality, but it enhances them, in order to achieve society's objectives (the duality of civilisation and well-being).

Yehya agreed with the general concepts of justice, but he had another view with regard to the implementation of justice inside the organisation. He said: 'The great challenge is that justice is relative, and not easy to measure. What may be considered justice for one person may be injustice for another.' To overcome this challenge, RSCN developed different mechanisms that can help to clear the ambiguity in this regard without contradicting I.Theory. These are as follows:

1. Systems: RSCN has adopted, in a fully participatory approach, different systems that institutionalise justice as a daily practice in most aspects of its work, including the HR system, such as: salary scale, incentive systems, performance appraisal systems, staff training and development system, etc.
2. All RSCN systems are directly connected with decision-making mechanisms that require more than one person, e.g. staff selection. Staff are evaluated by at least three staff members, including the line manager. In addition, a training committee makes decisions about training and development programmes.
3. Transparency and good communication: RSCN's management communicates all decisions and minutes of meetings to all staff, in order for them to be aware of all decisions. This mechanism helps staff to feel safe – that they will not be exposed to sudden decisions made by a single person. It also helps to develop a trusting atmosphere between managers and staff.
4. Not being afraid of criticism: Staff are encouraged to provide feedback about any decision in a proper way and managers are obliged to hear feedback and respond to it positively.

Freedom and equality brings justice to life

But Rami had another idea. He agreed with what I had been saying about justice; and at the same time supported Yehya's idea of justice being relative. He eventually reached the conclusion that what we were talking about was how to create, implement and live the case of an actual spirit of justice within organisations. Rami says: 'In fact, comparing between freedom, justice and equality to define which is more applicable and related to the others was somehow taking us away from considering other techniques and measures that we use to guarantee achieving at least a minimum level of development of justice in our organisational culture.

'Such an orientation toward justice pertains to what we call psychosocial structures in societies, which have their own natures and contexts. Nevertheless, we cannot ignore any of the proposed ideas as they were all interrelated.'

Rami insisted, then, that 'justice is represented in the social structure of the organisation', which we wanted to reach. At the same time, he saw that if freedom (when managed and controlled to strike a certain balance between individual and group freedom) is coupled with equality in a manner that blends both elements into a single component, it will be manifested in the form of RSCN's performance measures and procedures. It was in that context that we might be integrating elements of psychology with elements of sociology inside the enterprise in a way that would lead to achieving a more human organisational culture, which is the ideal goal of management and transformation.

Rami continued: 'We still need to promote the values of freedom and equality, which will snowball to the extent that RSCN applies justice. That is when we can define justice as a result produced by the creation and implementation of those levels of ideal individual behaviour and commitment inside RSCN in a way that will be the spark that brings justice to life.'

Justice is a collective value

To reinforce the practice of justice at RSCN, Rami said: 'At the training section level, a number of vital points have been completed in order to ensure that justice is carried out in this process. In order to achieve these goals, a few steps have been taken, such as: selection of any trainees is made through a formal committee of RSCN that includes all key personnel, who normally would not select anyone out of personal interest or otherwise.'

To summarise, Rami said: 'Justice is a collective value that cannot be achieved inside RSCN except when the necessary climate of sincerity, clarity, equality, transparency and many other values fundamental to producing the proper environment to achieve justice is ensured.' I then pointed out that it was necessary to build systems to practise justice in the HR section in general, and in the Training Unit in particular. What Rami had mentioned was a step, but not the vital procedure to transform RSCN as a learning organisation. They appreciated that, and I then started my new task in this case application, to test out the results of applying the HR systems that I would develop in accordance with I.Theory concepts. I asked the co-operative inquiry team to meet on a weekly basis to review, develop and apply their systems.

SECOND ACTION PHASE: BUILDING SYSTEMS

First step: the values-managed organisation

In our first meeting to develop systems (August 2006), I focused on building a culture in RSCN based on values to enhance the Director General's slogan: 'A values-managed organisation'. I asked them to think about formulating a special charter to be based on values and RSCN's mission, and which the co-operative inquiry team would have to explain to the employees. From then on, all RSCN staff members, current and prospective, would have to read and sign the charter. After three meetings to discuss and review the

RSCN mission, we issued the following charter in the spirit of I.Theory. The finalised charter came into effect after being endorsed by the Acting Director General.

RSCN CHARTER

In the spirit of our belief in our institution's mission to preserve biodiversity and its integration with socio-economic development, including spreading environmental awareness which is supported by the entire region, we, the staff of RSCN, declare our adherence to the following work standards:

Individual responsibility:

1. *Each and every one of us will demonstrate a high level of individual responsibility towards our work by performing our work with complete mastery and skill that will be reflected in the end result.*

2. *Not to neglect our own self-advancement through our work and to put it at the disposal of RSCN.*

3. *Our ethics will stem from the values of our society, and we will exercise self-monitoring in the process.*

4. *The basis for our dealings with each other will be respect and appreciation, and we will respect all the groups we deal with in our world.*

Collective responsibility:

1. *To be loyal soldiers to the Royal Society for the Conservation of Nature and to refrain from any actions that might reflect negatively on its image – therefore, to deal with communities with integrity and not harm them by any appearance, conduct or action; and be professional in our dealings with other institutions in the spirit of our mission; deal with the public with co-operation and kindness; and prove to everyone that we are all working for one goal, embodied in RSCN's mission: the protection of nature.*

2. *Because we possess this integrity, we must distance ourselves from anything that might bring that integrity into question and not serve the hidden agendas of any outside elements – to achieve that, we must be sure not to accept personal gifts, favours or free trips; not indulge in personal dealings that compromise our mission; not use RSCN's name for personal gain; and be sure to avoid any conflict of interests.*

3. *In order to complete the picture, we need to appear decent and presentable at work; keep our offices clean, proper and smoking-free; make our offices a reflection of RSCN's mission; and create a quiet working environment that helps us to perform our work.*

4. *We must handle our financial assets with honesty, by refraining from any theft, cheating or lying; use RSCN's resources wisely; and make trust our motto in work, without precluding the possibility of verification.*

5. *The epitome of our collective responsibility is to fully co-operate in the development of our skills, by not withholding information or experience from anyone, but to lend a helping hand to any employee who needs it, aiming through that to elevate RSCN to the highest level of performance and skill.*

Environmental responsibility:

1. *Support the idea of recycling in all its forms.*

2. *Conserve in the use of water and electricity.*

3. *Maintain our cars free of smoke exhaust.*

4. *Get rid of waste.*

5. *Contribute to any activity aimed at protecting the environment in general and biodiversity in particular.*

This charter is based on the faith and taqwa. If people have faith and taqwa, they will behave accordingly and exercise self-control in any job they do.

Second step: human resources management and I.Theory

One month later, I reviewed the RSCN employees' reaction to the charter with the co-operative inquiry team. It appeared that the individual reactions were positive. We also received positive reactions from new employees attending the induction course, which covers the RSCN charter. The most important thing was that the charter was built up via a participatory approach and complied with the mission of RSCN. However, there was a small percentage of people who were not interested in the charter. They were looking for any other job, if it meant more incentives or greater salaries. Those people ultimately quit RSCN.

After that, we started reviewing the application of I.Theory in the HR department. I asked about the selection and recruitment system.

Raja' said: 'We have no fixed systems, but generally we place ads for jobs in newspapers with the specific qualifications, skills and experience if necessary; then we conduct the interviews to select the person who has all the requirements that we need.'

Yehya said: 'In our selection and recruitment we are very transparent, and refuse any Wasta (favouritism).'

I said: 'I appreciate your enthusiasm in management, but we need some systems to practise justice and transparency when you select people. There are two important factors, strength of commitment and honesty in approach.' Many subsequent meetings were conducted to explain the philosophy of effectiveness in performance and link it with I.Theory. I explained how, first of all, it depends on an ongoing evaluation throughout the year, and records and explores the most important positive and negative issues concerning the employee.

At this point we turned purposefully to the knowledge modes.

SECOND REFLECTION PHASE: THE KNOWLEDGE MODES

Experiential knowledge bearing upon I.Theory

Enas started as a volunteer in the research section; after a short period there was a need for a researcher in the section to work on the biodiversity database. Two years later, she received training on GIS and later became responsible for it. She participated in some baseline surveys (survey design, fieldwork and reporting). In addition, she was able to help the Section Head with some managerial and financial tasks. When the position of Section Head became vacant, she applied for it, was interviewed and later on employed. As Section Head, her main responsibility at first was to re-build the section after two of its main researchers resigned and left Jordan for managerial positions in the field of conservation, thus leaving a vacancy in GIS in addition to the change in the position of Section Head.

The research team is now complete and work is under way to build the capacity of its staff, strengthen the team spirit and transfer knowledge to the new staff. More and more managerial tasks are required and the responsibility is increasing.

In the beginning, Enas's involvement was restricted to technical issues and reporting. Her involvement increased as she gained more experience. Meetings, workshops and presentations allowed her to give more and to be more involved in the decision-making process at the section level, at the conservation division level and recently at RSCN level and as a representative of RSCN in governmental organisations, NGOs and wherever required.

I asked her about the management style she adopts in her work, and why.

Enas said that while her background was non-managerial, 'I learnt a few things by watching other managers, and I gained more knowledge through training workshops on basic managerial skills. But the biggest source of knowledge came through the few months of practice I had, when there was no manager in the section. I started reading about management styles but did not adopt any specific system. Sometimes I draw upon and focus on the theme of teamwork in the Japanese model to enhance team spirit. In other cases, I use a different approach to deal with individuals with special talents.

'All management values applied are based on the belief that the work and all what we do is a responsibility and *Amanah* (trust) and that God will ask us about each and every word, act and decision we take. Nevertheless, in a society like RSCN that deals with different sectors of society, from locals to NGOs and decision-makers, RSCN has to take some actions and decisions according to the Japanese model or the Western model, according to the specificity of the decision.'

We then switched our attention from the experiential, via Enas, to the imaginal, in this case via Rami.

Imaginal knowledge bearing on I.Theory

With his belief in transformation management, as a methodology and its content, Rami reflected the same view as that held by the Director General. He believed strongly that change is the main path for creation; thus, RSCN staff should always think about transformation in principle, which he believes leads to creating what we today call 'transformation management'. But how can that be done?

Rami said: 'We need to conduct an institutional analysis of strengths and weaknesses to detect areas in need of improvement in order to design a building and development plan based on tangible and solid facts pertaining to needs, which normally requires having a deeper understanding of human performance and attitudes. For that, we need to adopt ethics that would enable them to imagine the approach and philosophy necessary for achieving their move towards change and creating the required level of spirit and performance to achieve transformation – a transformation that is considered a major tool that can be used in any institution to help it create its own culture.'

With regard to the relationship between quality and Islam, Rami said: 'They both espouse the same major values and ethics. Since its inception, I.Theory has been seeking to disseminate a number of ethics and values that will always lead to creating an environment conducive to increasing the quality of human life, performance and behaviour. The same applies to recent quality standards aimed at increasing human performance and reactions. But even those standards do not rise up to the level of Islam, which has struck a real balance between different motivational performance factors. Islam did the same when it strove to accumulate and integrate all major elements of performance (such as affiliation, power and achievement) to create a strong move towards change. The proof of that explanation is that Islam, at the time of the Prophet, who was duly inspired by Allah, was able to achieve the highest levels of change within the shortest period of time, which confirms and indicates a very strong policy of change that was able to accomplish the fastest and highest quantum leap in society.'

Conceptual knowledge and its bearing on I.Theory

Co-operative inquiry at RSCN has affinities with the action research approach and the associated experiential learning arising from the work of Kurt Lewin, whereby: 'In action research, all actors involved in the research process are equal participants, and must be involved in every stage of the research process. Collaborative participation in theoretical, practical, and political discourse is a hallmark of action research and the action researcher' (Heron, 1996)

During one of my meetings with the co-researchers, we explored their role in implementing I.Theory, and their actual reactions.

For Yehya: 'We need to trust that the top management has employees' best interest at heart. We also need to make justice the ultimate value at RSCN. How do we protect this ultimate value? Do we need a special committee to make sure justice is served?'

He added: 'We implement justice as an ultimate value. When we recruited our employees at RSCN, some considered this process the opposite of justice; therefore, we have to develop our systems to guarantee justice among all our employees.'

Enas: 'We have been talking a lot. If we believe that there is no justice, then we cannot achieve progress. However, there is a problem; we need closer relationships among all employees, and among employees and stakeholders.

'The problem is that we need a better communication system between the employees and senior management. If we do that, we will achieve justice as an ultimate value.'

Mohammad Qawaba': 'We have another problem, which is giving the opportunity to all employees to communicate directly with the executive committee without overstepping their direct managers!'

Yehya: 'The executive committee allows people to see its decisions, but our employees do not care. They do not know what they want. We need a decision to transfer an employee to another job instead of terminating his employment at RSCN.'

I.Theory, in principle, achieves unification between the employees and the organisation. How can we guarantee that? What are RSCN's rights? How can we evaluate them? What are RSCN employees' rights? If we can answer the above questions, we will achieve the implementation of I.Theory.

Practical knowledge and its bearing on I.Theory

Yehya said: 'We now have to know how we can achieve that balance … We need an RSCN charter (code of ethics), and a general system to protect the rights of both parties. Our objective is to have that unification between the organisation (RSCN) and the employees. RSCN now has a charter (code of ethics) and is applying systems. We are performing the transformation process based on our culture and religion. I cannot claim it is a complete I.Theory, but we are trying to build and construct the best that we can. Also I can confirm the following results:

- 'People's commitment towards values and the organisation, which enhanced their participation in all processes at RSCN.
- 'High efficiency in performance and quality.
- 'Enhanced trust of RSCN by governmental institutions.
- 'Most employees are participating in any activity to solve problems or take decisions, which reflects the trust between employees and the top management.'

  We then turned from the epistemic (knowledge modes) to the political.

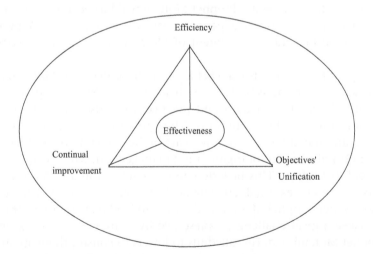

Figure 10.1 The I.Theory effectiveness value

Democracy and participation (Shura), RSCN and I.Theory

I conducted further meetings with the co-operative inquiry team during September and October 2006, to discuss RSCN as a non-governmental organisation (NGO), their perceptions of this NGO and how it had developed. Yehya said the following about RSCN as an NGO (his historical and observational points of view):

- 'The concept of civil society is relatively recent because it only appeared in the twentieth century, especially in Arab countries. Therefore, we rarely find literature about the experience of civil society in Arab countries.
- 'Civil society has a strategic weakness: it suffers from an identity crisis. At the time when it is emerging as a third global power, alongside business and government, civil society has no clear idea of its distinct identity and the sources of its strengths and weaknesses.
- 'If Europe was the first to proclaim that the world was made by culture, and that 'doing culture' is thereby a human job, then doing culture is a human job done in groups, not individually, and that is what history has been demonstrating so far. Organisations represent a form of group that has to develop a culture; otherwise, they will become extinct, like other past civilisations.
- 'The great Nelson Mandela would not have succeeded in establishing the new South Africa, without a new democratic constitution (public), the work of the renowned Truth and Reconciliation Commission (civic) and a resilient business community (private). I can confidently say: "I will not be able to succeed without strong support from the public (civic), a modern financial system that facilitates the operation of the organisation and a unified team who share the same values."
- 'Institutions have to be established and developed based on the noble values of society. We saw how successful Prophet Mohammad has been in achieving that, and how the Japanese and Chinese experience was successful as well. We need to do that in order to continue the development of RSCN as a leading organisation in Arab countries.
- 'The concept of *taqwa* (God-fearing behaviour) can be developed into an institutional value: a sense of responsibility. The teachings of Islam emphasise individual responsibility in matters of faith and practice; they also stress the importance of responsibility towards the community. The Qur'an and the Sunnah (the Prophet's tradition) contain many rules on how to act in life – what to do and what not to do.
- 'There is a fifth dimension for organisation management, which can be characterised as a fivefold institution. This new dimension requires the internal team to support managers in facing external challenges. The following story explains the new dimension: When Prophet Mohammad moved to Medina to establish the first Islamic state, he faced a great challenge, represented by non-believers attacking Medina to fight Prophet Mohammad. He called his followers to consult them about the matter. The followers responded positively to his request: "We will not tell you to go you and your God to fight the enemy while we wait here. We will join you and your God in fighting the enemy."'

I told him that we were all with him in this long, transformational journey, and I was looking for success.

Figure 10.2 reflects the external environment, which includes the political, cultural, economic and natural elements; but in order to link between them, we need the internal supportive environment, which means values (values-managed organisations, in this case), because without values we cannot co-ordinate between the four elements. The internal supportive environmental here is based on I.Theory, with values at its core.

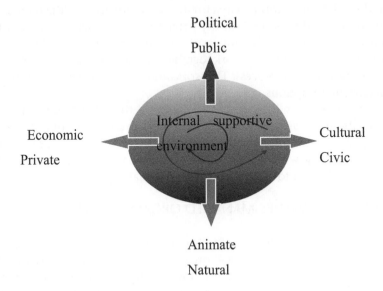

Figure 10.2 Fivefold institutional model

Source: M.Sc., third project, University of Buckingham/Yehya Khaled

Towards a 'Fivefold Institution'

SETTING A PROCESS IN MOTION

Yehya realised that the transformation process towards a 'fivefold institution' is a long-term process that would not achieve its objectives without real commitment from all the staff at RSCN. Therefore, he has tried to set in motion a process that will enable RSCN to meet this long-term goal and achieve the initial 'buy-in' from the staff. In developing this process, he has drawn upon the various theories to create his own approach to institutional development. His plan included the following:

1. Developing institutional responsibility at RSCN, including transforming RSCN into a values-managed organisation.
2. Effective use of private sector tools to help the organisation achieve its objectives.
3. Introducing new mechanisms for interaction with the public.
4. Developing new mechanisms to demonstrate RSCN's social responsibility.

However, Yehya could not achieve the above goals without the practice and implementation of the core justice value, both within and outside RSCN, following I.Theory. 'We also believe in the alignment between quality, Islam and transformation, because Islam can help to integrate quality with transformation.'

PROMOTING TEAM SUPPORT FOR THE TRANSFORMATION PROCESS

To maximise the benefit of the transformation process and make sure that its impact goes deeper into the RSCN institution, Yehya invited all senior and middle managers at RSCN, representing different disciplines and departments, to an orientation workshop on the new concepts of institutional development and their potential implications for RSCN. The objective was for the group to work together to shape the management of RSCN and facilitate the transformation process. The workshop was an initial opportunity to explore different management options.

The results of these reflections led to building the HR systems based on values-managed organisations, with the values system and the core value of justice at the centre. Of special importance in this regard is the evaluation system based on the effectiveness of the concept of I.Theory, which also calls for continual improvement based on creativity and initiative, in addition to experience and continual learning.

INTRODUCING THE 'VALUES-MANAGED ORGANISATION'

Over three days during April 2006, 46 RSCN managers discussed a wide range of concepts and theories related to 'values-managed organisations' and I.Theory. The team agreed to adopt I.Theory and the HR systems that follow accordingly, with a view to transforming RSCN into a values-managed organisation. I.Theory needs to identify the core value of the organisation as the main building block for developing all of the organisation's culture and systems. Moreover, in order to guarantee employees' commitment to the organisation's values and to secure employee participation in the process of value development, it is necessary to derive these values from society's culture, nature and religions.

RSCN's core values were developed as a result of two processes: firstly a *values identification session*. In this session, 46 managers of different RSCN departments held serious discussions about the organisation's core values and the most suitable one for RSCN. Rami shared his: 'My work values depend on fairness, equal distribution of development chances, positive thinking styles and team spirit. My Islamic beliefs are all based on one major belief: God's omnipresence and omniscience, He is always watching even when no one else is. This belief makes me always careful with what I say and do, especially where it concerns others, such as my institution: RSCN. Enas, also as a team leader, believes that all management values need to be based on *Amanah* (honesty), and that "God will hold us accountable for each and every word, act and decision".'

I sensed that there was great willingness to realise justice, in spite of all the difficulties that it met.

For Nash'at: 'Justice means ensuring that everyone's rights are respected according to Islamic beliefs, in addition to being more flexible, honest, and easy going, but to have very clear and straight principles that are not negotiable.'

Secondly, I drew on a questionnaire about RSCN core values and work ethics.

The majority of RSCN employees indicated that they wanted '*Taqwa* – the sense of responsibility' to be the core value. Further analysis of employees' responses indicated that the core value could be divided into four sub-values:

1. Sense of responsibility for individual actions
2. Sense of responsibility for the group destiny
3. Responsibility for continuous development
4. Responsibility to conserve biodiversity and protect the environment.

'How do we go about creating "values-managed organisations"?' Yehya Khaled raised this question during the meeting in April 2006 with the 46 managers at RSCN. All of them agreed that we needed to implement I.Theory accordingly. This approach is based on the I.Theory that dictates identifying the core value for the organisation and the main building blocks for developing all management systems.

DEVELOPING INNOVATIVE WAYS TO EXPRESS THESE NEW VALUES

Ultimately, value statements are merely words. To acquire meaning, values must be reflected in the actions of the organisation and the behaviour of its members. If a personal sense of accountability and responsibility is not deep and strong enough, then all legislative and executive actions and intellectual support will fail. In order to overcome this problem and reduce the gap between values of rhetoric and values of behaviour, the Acting Director General developed a mechanism to bridge the gap and give the agreed core values a practical meaning in working life at RSCN, based on society's language, culture, nature and religion.

In June 2006 he invited 30 staff members representing all RSCN workplaces, and asked them to sit in groups according to their workplace. He then asked them to find the best way to express RSCN's values in words, pictures or drawings that could inspire them continuously and enhance their commitment to these values.

WHAT IS THE FUTURE OF RSCN?

Yehya: 'RSCN is an evolving organism which responds positively to the outside environment and opportunities, otherwise RSCN will become extinct.'

So, Yehya sees that the future of RSCN linked with radical transformation.

Enas: 'The short notice for beginning to implement the transformation process systems, the load of work, the lack of a team with a full understanding of the concept and the absence of a full picture among managers as to what the process is, is a factor in slowing the process of transformation. But the changes accomplished so far are good. But the process still needs time and effort.'

Yehya: 'With regard to RSCN's future, I would like to be more optimistic. I can see it expanding quickly, especially with the project of the Integrated Ecosystem Management in the Rift Valley on the way, and the fact that at least Burgu will be established in the eastern desert. I am sure that with RSCN's systems and regulations and the efforts of the staff, correct management will take place. But I can see neglect in building team spirit and relationships between employees; and for an NGO like RSCN, working in the conservation of nature and for a cause, relationships between the employees, management, society and local communities play a major role in working out all the problems we face at work.'

Rami: 'I can say that a number of major changes have been made to achieve this vision; but still, I am not fully aware of specific changes that were the target of that transformation. This does not allow me to be completely sure as to how much has been achieved up till now. But as to RSCN's future: I see it filled with potential and responsibilities, which requires the immediate development of a long-term future plan based on the most accurate management style available, which will achieve the required level of performance and will also be the ideal basis for the spirit and values that will guarantee the targeted performance.'

Linking the future of RSCN back to I.Theory – systemically

The next co-operative meeting was held at RSCN after a call from Yehya, who asked me to help them focus on career-path and succession systems. Rami, Raja' and As'ad attended this meeting.

Maqbouleh: 'Back to our first subject: what is the effect of the Islamic theory on achieving quality, as you are aware by now of the elements and systems of I.Theory in management. I see that the quality concept in RSCN's services revolves around work and lifestyle. The most important application of I.Theory is in building systems aimed at transforming our people; we need to build systems to enhance relationships among them. What HR systems do you have? Yehya asked me to build a career-path system. Do you have a grading system for every job title at RSCN? How do you build up organisational structures and processes accordingly?'

Raja: 'We started with new job descriptions and training needs assessment. Rami asked me to re-build all systems from scratch because he felt that they needed radical change to achieve transformation and values and implement their charter.'

The components of HR were now to be established, I said, according to the RSCN core value of justice. This meant that they had to observe the following criteria:

1. Fairness – paying wages commensurate with work.
2. Levels in salary scales should not be too wide apart.
3. The minimum wage should be congruent with the requirements of a decent standard of living.

Rami: 'I hope we reach that stage; but from my experience, salaries do not reflect the effort made at all managerial levels. So, I do not feel that they are just or fair.'

Raja' saw the converse; she said: 'We now have the flexibility to make any amendment for any employee.'

Again I raised other aspects. 'If you want to motivate employees and deepen their commitment to group goals, most important, according to I.Theory, are:

- 'To focus on satisfaction, not fulfilment.
- 'To group together positive, as opposed to negative, motivations.
- 'To motivate people on both an individual and a group basis.
- 'The best motivation is shared between employees and the organisation.'

So what point had RSCN reached, at this stage, in I.Theory terms?

STAGES OF THE INQUIRY REVISITED

Towards strength and honesty

Rami: 'We have to change our culture to focus more on satisfaction – not fulfilment.'

Raja': 'We have differences amounting to 10 times in salaries between the lowest or highest paid employees. And our incentives are based on MBO, as you see in the performance appraisal form. We have recently linked our incentive system with individuals and groups, but it was only implemented once this year for groups.'

I asked our co-researchers about the system of promotion at RSCN, especially in connection with *aya* 11 of *sura* Al-Mujadalah (She Who Disputes): *'God will raise those of you who believe, and those who have knowledge.'*

There are, in I.Theory terms, two bases for promotion:

- Faith – considered the ultimate indicator for the set of total values
- Knowledge –the second rule for promotion, which, along with faith, represents the duality of faith–knowledge.

Rami and Raja' indicated that the promotional system was based on shared values (faith in RSCN) and knowledge, amongst other things.

Finally, I wanted to focus on the conditions of recruitment and selection. I knew that RSCN and the Acting Director General are against *Wasta* (nepotism) and consider it a form of corruption. In addition, Allah focuses on this point in *sura* Al-Qasas (The Narration), *aya* 26: *'Surely the best man to employ is one who is strong and honest.'* This verse covers the following two conditions of recruitment and selection:

- Strength – includes both physical and intellectual strength
- Honesty – as a value, which means that a human being can be trusted.

What is the state at RSCN with regard to these concepts, and how are they related to I.Theory?

The selection and recruitment system at RSCN is as follows, Raja' said: 'We identify the specification of the employee needed, and put an advertisement in the newspaper. Then we study all the documents and start arranging for interviews. We hire the best, based on qualifications, experience and values. So, we use the I.Theory requirement, which is to recruit the strongest and most honest.'

For Yehya: 'What happened between you and Dr Assaf in adopting I.Theory, as developed by you both, is much better than if we start the process alone. Now we need more to put our staff on the right track.'

For Enas: 'The changes that have happened so far are good, but we believe that the process needs time and effort. For me, I think that more attention should have been given to promoting employees' attachment to and faith in RSCN, generally, and I.Theory, specifically.'

For Rami: 'We cannot guarantee that what is happening in reality was actually what was intended at this point.' He also mentioned certain partial measures based on a few Islamic principles that had been established.

For Nash'at: 'Yes of course, it's complex: Islamic management theory comes between Western individualism and Japanese socialism.'

As for Yehya, he felt that there was no consensus in this respect. At the same time, he indicated that the majority encouraged using the principles of Islam and of Jordanian culture to develop RSCN's management.

Rami stressed that RSCN was taking its first baby steps towards achieving such concepts or approach because that process was completely dependent on individual readiness. But there was still a gap at this stage, requiring further action and development in order to reach the basis of co-operation in theory and practice.

By this stage, overall, there was a feeling that, with the pre-emphasis of I.Theory on justice, RSCN needed to turn its attention to society at large.

Towards fair trade: RSCN's socio-economic role in Jordan

RSCN recognises that social and economic forces are the major causes in compromising the ecosystem's integrity, involving:

- poverty and inequity
- trade and uncontrolled globalisation
- wealth and consumption.

To reverse these effects, a new vision has to emerge to secure living in a healthy environment, along with wider understanding of and respect for the environment, in its broadest sense, including its natural, social, economic and cultural aspects. With that end in mind, RSCN decided to play an active role in the Fair Trade movement.

What are the rules of Fair Trade, and how can RSCN develop the community?

Yehya said: 'Unfortunately, the rules are rigged to benefit the rich and marginalise the poor. Fair Trade is an attempt to reverse that bias. It is not going to fix the global system. That will take major institutional changes and a determined campaign.'

Producers are paid a fair price and workers a fair wage. For crops like coffee, tea and bananas, farmers are paid a stable minimum price whereby, specifically: the links between buyers and sellers are shortened, doing away with 'middle men'; buyers and producers develop long-term relationships of mutual support and benefit; all aspects of the trading relationship are open to public accountability; exploitative child labour and forced labour are prohibited; working conditions are healthy and safe; goods are produced and crops grown in an environmentally sustainable way.

A consortium was formalised between the biggest three organisations working in the field of biodiversity, conservation and human development: the World Conservation Union, Jordanian Hashemite Fund for Human Development and RSCN to form Fair Trade Jordan to fulfil the following objectives:

Goal: To manage Jordan's resources (renewable and non-renewable) sustainably and distribute benefits equitably.

Purpose: To establish in Jordan a Fair Trade institutional structure that promotes the sustainable use of natural resources, contributes to social equity and poverty reduction and ensures improved market access to Fair Trade products and services.

Operational objectives:

- Develop 'Fair Trade' products
- Promote the use of resources sustainably and 'fairly'
- Understand 'Fair Trade' customers
- Provide access to 'Fair Trade' markets
- Help producers meet 'Fair Trade' standards
- Guarantee fair returns to small producers.

The consortium represents an umbrella for Fair Trade activities in Jordan. It has so far facilitated several activities, including:

- Conducting several workshops to promote learning about the concepts among producers and stakeholders.
- Successful organisation of a National Forum on Euro-Med Partnership.
- Inviting more than 100 producers from Jordan, Lebanon, Palestine and Yemen to exhibit their products in Wild Jordan.

We are now ready to conclude the RSCN case study, and the application of I.Theory in relation to it.

Conclusion

STARTING WITH EXPERIENTIAL KNOWLEDGE

Through my concluding discussions with the co-operative inquiry team at RSCN, and after two years of implementation and living through this process, technically and culturally, we were able to reflect on the four modes of co-operative inquiry bearing upon I.Theory, specifically in relation to transformation and quality.

The experiential mode, to begin with, encompasses feeling and emotion, which means the intense, localised effect that arises from the fulfilment or frustration of individual needs. By feeling, Heron refers to the capacity of the psyche to participate in wider unities of being. This is the domain of empathy, indwelling, participation, presence, resonance and so on, bearing, in our case, on the exercise of justice, in terms both of people and of nature.

In RSCN, love of nature is shared by everyone in the co-operative inquiry team. This leads on to loving the organisation, protecting nature and doing one's best at work to propagate such love in all rural communities. So without the experiential/affective mode, embracing feeling and emotion, we could not see that kind of struggle to protect our nature through our culture. Through this mode, RSCN has also drawn upon the staff's emotionally laden, religious convictions to promote faith in RSCN.

ENTERING THE IMAGINAL MODE

The imaginal mode comprises intuition and imagery, which means the capacity of the psyche to generate an individual viewpoint, a unique outlook on life through the use of living imagery. Heron refers here to the immediate comprehensive knowing whereby the mind can grasp a field, a system or being as a patterned unity. It is continuously creative, it generates imagery through perception and creative imagination. So the imaginal mind is interpenetrative, participative and fundamentally collective.

As such, the imaginal mode implemented at RSCN was reflected, overall, in the participative management style that the senior management followed towards quality and transformation, and the role of management by values in charting such development. Moreover, ecologists have rubbed shoulders with Bedouin, interweaving local and global knowledge to develop new, natural products, all across RSCN's sites in Jordan. This has required a mix of 'feminine' empathy and 'masculine' ingenuity. From an Islamic perspective, Allah said in *sura* Al-Hujurat (The Private Apartments), *aya* 13: '*O human, we created you from a male and a female, and we made you races and tribes for you to get to know each other.*'

Moreover, RSCN has created a new image for itself as a knowledge-creating organisation, by building on the historical *Beit Al-Hikma*/House of Wisdom in Baghdad during the Islamic golden age. It sees itself now offering knowledge to all the neighbouring countries, such as Syria, Lebanon, Arab Emirates and others. This regional role has encouraged RSCN to work locally–globally; and it was awarded an international Green Apple Environment Award, in recognition of its environmental good practice in conducting the 'Save Jordan Trees' advocacy campaign. The award was presented to the RSCN in the House of Commons, London, on 20 November 2006.

THE CONCEPTUAL MODE: RSCN'S MISSION AND STRATEGY

We now turn, thirdly, to the conceptual mode, which includes reflection and making distinctions, involving the ability to categorise things, distinguish between one thing and another and identify similarities and differences by reflection. Heron refers to the experience of thinking in general terms. This is the domain of models, systems, laws and theories. I.Theory, as a management concept, is one such. Once this is appreciated, it becomes possible for knowledge to uncover the *essence* of matters. Elaborating on the conceptual mode, in relation to RSCN, entailed a lot of action and subsequent reflection, gathering evidence, suggestions, expressions and signs. The RSCN Charter represented a summation of what we might term the organisation's mission and strategy, as follows (Appendix 2):

> In 2005, RSCN launched its new strategy, including its new mission 'to conserve biodiversity in Jordan and integrate its conservation with economic development and gain more public support and action for environmental protection in Jordan and the neighbouring countries.' Everyone thought this was a dream that could not be turned into reality. Today, we are proud to say the RSCN has made huge steps towards fulfilling this mission.

> Protected Areas were always seen as the main vehicle for fulfilling the RSCN's noble mission, but in the past they faced much resistance from the locals because they were seen as intruding on people's rights without bringing any tangible benefits to them. In 1993, the RSCN renewed its management for protected areas and for the first time introduced the concept of linking biodiversity conservation with economic development through the Dana Project.

This new approach was extremely successful in changing the image of protected areas, from isolated islands benefiting only the elite, to multi-purpose assets where nature is integrated with community and economic needs. Instead of imposing a blanket prohibition on access, certain areas are zoned for conservation and others for public use through careful management. The RSCN further developed the concept of eco-friendly business, in the new millennium, in protected areas as represented by socio-economic programmes and ecotourism. Today, these eco-friendly businesses are bringing tangible economic benefits to the local communities and the country as a whole.

All these steps lie at the heart of the unifying notion behind I.Theory, that is, between individuals, groups and community.

THE PRACTICAL MODE: RSCN PRODUCTS AND SERVICES

RSCN's protected areas today are being managed efficiently to maintain dynamic ecosystems and habitats and embrace their needs, even when this requires initiatives outside their boundaries. It has become common practice to integrate biodiversity conservation measures within different land use practices, such as agriculture and mass tourism developments. We can see the results of this integrated approach in the recovery of many wild animal and plant populations throughout Jordan.

These results have not have been achieved by conservation efforts alone. They also reflect the new generation of Jordanians who, for the last 30 years, have been exposed to intensive environmental and awareness programmes and to modern advocacy approaches that have helped to influence policies and legislation in favour of biodiversity conservation.

RSCN, moreover, has long realised it will not be able to fulfil its role effectively and efficiently unless it remains a strong and dynamic institution, capable of responding to increasing responsibilities. The high level of qualification of the staff and their commitment to RSCN's cause has made the greatest contribution to its achievements to date. RSCN believes, finally, that nature conservation and economic development can go hand in hand.

It also believes that Jordan's nature can provide the basis of an alternative economy for members of poor rural communities who currently have few opportunities to improve their livelihoods.

More specifically, in that practical respect, RSCN:

- runs special programmes to save endangered species
- sets up protected areas to safeguard wildlife and scenic areas of Jordan
- carries out research to provide a scientific base for its conservation work
- controls illegal hunting and helps to enforce other wildlife laws
- raises awareness through school education programmes, media coverage, publications and special campaigns
- creates jobs and new economic opportunities for members of rural communities through eco-tourism, craft production and nature-based business
- provides training and capacity building for environmental practitioners and other institutions throughout Jordan and the Middle East

- encourages public participation and advocacy through membership, local forums, events and activities.

The practical mode involves intention and action, which reflect individual acts and the personal responsibility level, to generate the world of *existence*. Intention and action are primary and, together with emotion and feeling, create a lived world of enterprise and endeavour in which deeds encounter what exists. At the practical level, this enterprise includes all kinds of experimental and action research, as well as industry in general. At the effective level, it has the nature of interpersonal encounter and relationship, of voyages and journeys: the heart and the will take us forth to meet particular people and places. Between these levels, at the centre of the world of existence, lie patterns of propositions and practices. Here RSCN has been furthering its co-operation with the private sector, using the sector's experience to develop and update its financial policies and procedures and provide professional performance services to RSCN, which is being done by a consulting firm specialised in financial management. The firm has reviewed all RSCN's financial operations, identified weaknesses on the basis on this analysis and proposed new policies and procedures to overcome these weaknesses.

RSCN AND I.THEORY

I.Theory does not impose pre-defined instructions or rules on and for people. Rather, it presents a framework based on the core value of justice, which underlies effectiveness, inside the organisation, leading to continuous improvement. In terms of co-operative inquiry, as instigated in the RSCN case:

- The experiential element of justice is embodied in the empathetic relationship and close-knit relationships with people and with nature.
- The imaginal element is contained within the image of unity and interdependence, which underlies creation.
- The conceptual element is encompassed in conservation management and the management of biodiversity, not only ecologically and culturally, but also socially and politically, doing justice to each, as it were.
- Finally, practically, the exercise of justice, in the way RSCN is constituted, embodying fairness, and incorporating mutual rights and responsibilities, is duly manifest.

I will now turn to the second case study, Al-Quds Paints Co., to see how it is developing its business and creating an Islamic culture through implementing Islamic values, in this case within a private enterprise.

CHAPTER 11

Case Study 2: Al-Quds Paints Co. – Amman/Jordan

Introduction

FROM CIVIC TO PRIVATE ENTERPRISE

In the previous chapter I described how, in the application of I.Theory to RSCN, a civic and environmentally based enterprise, I drew upon co-operative inquiry as my informative–transformative approach. I was working with a managing director who was himself a graduate of our master's in Transformation Management course, through which we have been exposed to the integral approach of TRANS4M. Al Quds Paints Co. was a very different story, in that its managing director had no such prior exposure. In fact, it was I.Theory itself to which he was drawn.

I had worked with RSCN during 2005–6, while heavily engaged in my doctoral studies. My work with Al Quds Paints Co. began in 2008, when my studies were coming to an end. My work with it involved a fully fledged organisational development in 2008, and a follow-up in 2009 in order to see how the application of I.Theory had, or had not, transformed the company in the space of one year. During the follow-up process I again used the co-operative inquiry method, and formed a team of co-researchers accordingly.

THE COMPANY HISTORY

Al-Quds Paints Co. (Jerusalem Paints Co.) was established in Amman, Jordan in 1994, under the name Jerusalem Paints Industries, as a family business headed by Jamil Jubran. He had been working in for some years with another paints company when he decided to establish Al-Quds Paints as a family-owned manufacturing business with its own brand. The company started with two lines of product: water-based interior wall putty and cement-based tile adhesive.

The production volume was modest: the total daily production of both products was 200 units. In 2003, local sales increased, with year-on-year growth of 30 per cent; by

2008/–9 the company had a daily production capacity of 6,000 units of its traditional putty and tile adhesive products.

WHY AL-QUDS PAINTS CO.?

Being of Palestinian origin, it was important for the Jubran family to choose the name Al-Quds Paints Co., in order to reflect a geopolitical and spiritual need. The city of Al-Quds (Arabic for Jerusalem) has a symbolic value, for its Arabic and Islamic architecture and colours. Furthermore, despite their local production, most of the paint companies in Jordan have foreign names, such as 'National', 'American' and so on. Al-Quds Paints Co. is the first business in Jordan to use an authentically Arabic brand name for locally produced paints.

The father, Jamil Jubran, wanted Al-Quds Paints Co. to be inspired by the family's roots and a by place of origin with profound meaning for his family's future, for both financial and social reasons.

So how to combine spiritual, financial and social needs in Al-Quds Paints Co.? Jamil Jubran gave the answer: 'By ensuring an exceptional quality, reasonable cost and an excellent service.' He added: 'Many people advised us to stop our project of building Al-Quds Paints because the market had suppliers who practised ruthless competition. However, something was missing, which justified setting up Al-Quds Paints, and expanding it in terms of employees and in relation to the surrounding environment.'

STARTING MY CO-OPERATION WITH AL-QUDS PAINTS CO.

Amer Jubran is the eldest of Jamil Jubran's sons, and is currently the General Manager of Al-Quds Paints Co. In 2008 he visited me at my office and asked me to do a consultancy assignment for him. He wanted to develop the company and its employees so as to create a corporate culture based on its roots. He believed in transformation and had a vision for making the company one of the top five in Jordan.

I said: 'Great, I can help you – on one condition: if you will give me your commitment, time and co-operation in this long transformation process focused on values-managed organisation.' In fact, Amer Jubran attended many workshops that I held with key people in the factory about the importance of quality (*Itqan*) and, of course, of I.Theory.

THE UNDERLYING RATIONALE FOR TRANSFORMATION

There were many reasons, in fact, that led Al-Quds Paints Co. to start this transformation process, such as:

1. The General Manager is highly educated and open minded. He knows how to deal with his employees, and believes in Islamic values and their impact on people's way of life.
2. The two brothers of the General Manager are working in the company, the one as Marketing Manager and the other as Production Manager. Both deal with the workers as partners. The two attended many of my workshops about values-managed organisation, and Islamic values in particular.

3. An open-door policy is encouraged, and regular meetings are held between senior management and staff.
4. Al-Quds Paints Co.'s objectives are to achieve quality (*Itqan*), to become one of the top manufacturers in Jordan and to increase market share, in addition to entering new regional and international markets. Realising these objectives requires effort and commitment, especially in view of the existing competition and unstable markets.

THE CONSULTING AGENDA: WORK AS WORSHIP

The consulting assignment helped me to focus on the implementation of Islamic values, such as regarding work as a form of worship, and the quality (*Itqan*) of work as an order of the Prophet (Peace be upon him). This raised the following questions, analogous to those I had pursued with RSCN, but now in a very different context:

a) How can we develop a management theory based on our Islamic values that leads to enhanced quality and transformation?
b) What is the role of I.Theory in supporting the development of quality management and transformation?

I followed all the steps used in the RSCN case, based on John Heron's methodology of co-operative inquiry and Robert Yin's case study.

Setting the Scene

THE CAST OF CHARACTERS

The following, to begin with, are the profiles of the co-operative inquiry team members who were involved:

Amer Jubran: General Manager/Partner: Born in 1969 into a Palestinian refugee family, he grew up in Jordan after the second Arab–Israeli war in 1967. He did his elementary and secondary studies in a government school in Amman.

'Wake up son. You should come with me to work.' With these words he was introduced to the world of paints at the beginning of his school summer holidays in 1983. At the time, Amer did not know what the word 'work' meant, or what paints did. It was a new territory for him.

In 1987, he went to the USA to study, and in 1993 got a bachelor's degree in Business Administration from North Eastern University. After obtaining his degree, he returned to Jordan to help carry out his father's idea of establishing the Al-Quds Paints factory. 'The hard work of building a manufacturing entity with a brand belonging to the Jubran family has started,' Amer said. Amer then decided to gain more experience to help him face the challenges of being a Deputy Manager, so he returned to the USA, where he worked for four years in car sales and for three years as a Programme Manager to qualify medical translators. After seven years, Amer returned to Jordan to manage the factory with full delegation from his father.

Samer Jubran: Marketing Manager/Partner: Gained a bachelor's degree in Chemistry from Yarmouk University, Jordan in 1994. He started work in the factory immediately after graduation. He developed his skills in sales and marketing through many training courses, such as in marketing strategy, sales skills, negotiation skills, quality and environmental management, and HR management and development. In 2004 he was promoted to Marketing Manager.

Maher Jubran: Production Manager/Partner: The youngest brother of the Jubran family, he started work at Al-Quds Paints after finishing his secondary education in 1995. He has attended many training courses to raise his competencies in paints production, such as in paints industry technology, quality control and quality assurance in the paints manufacturing process, and has also attended some managerial training courses in leadership, in negotiation skills and in strategic management.

Maher believes in Islamic values and this greatly influences the workers' behaviour. He emphasises the importance of work as a form of worship and adherence to the *Taqwa* value in work. He also has an important role in defining the relationships amongst everyone (management and employees) in the factory.

Ola Attiyeh: Quality Assurance Manager: Holds a bachelor's degree in Chemistry and has been working in the company for two years. Having confidence in her, the management has sent her to attend many technical courses abroad, such as paints industry technology, chemical and physical testing for all types of paints, internal auditing for quality systems, and quality and environmental management, in addition to quality assurance in the paints industry.

Ola Attiyeh worked with TEAM Jordan in building a Quality Management System ISO 9001, in 2008, and an Environment Management System ISO 14001. After the company had achieved the international certificates of ISO 9001 and ISO 14001, the General Manager, Amer Jubran, appointed her to be Quality Assurance Manager. She has various relationships with all departments and sections of the organisation, and reports to the General Manager directly.

Izzeddeen Abu Zir: Showroom Manager: Holds a high school diploma. He joined Al-Quds Paints Co. five years ago and has had five years of experience in a number of fields. His main work is to help customers select the paint colours that best meet their needs by providing them with appropriate advice. Due to the company's belief in enhancing its people's skills and in the importance of knowledge sharing, Izzeddeen Abu Zir has attended many courses, such as in sales techniques, negotiation skills, quality and environmental management. In 2009, the top management promoted him to Showroom Manager.

Haifa Abu Rabdeh: Purchasing Manager: Holds a high school diploma and joined Al-Quds Paints Co. three years ago as Executive Secretary. She was promoted to General Manager's Assistant after one year, and in 2009 became Purchasing Manager. She has seven years' experience in a chemical company as an Administrative Officer. She has found her niche in Al-Quds Paints, especially with her new promotion to Purchasing Manager. She always says: 'The environment at Al-Quds Paints Co. is a family atmosphere; and we all work for the company's growth.'

Salem Elrukab: Raw Material Store Officer: Holds a Vocational Diploma and joined Al-Quds Paints Co. four years ago. He has a seven years' previous experience. Salem has attended many training courses, especially in warehouse management and control, quality control in the paints industry and paints industrial technology. Salem says: 'With the training courses I increased my knowledge and my competencies.'

Khaled Abu Ermaise: Maintenance Officer: holds a Vocational Diploma and has been employed at Al-Quds Paints Co. for the past four years. He has attended many training courses to increase his skills and knowledge, such as in leadership skills, quality control in the paints industry and paints industrial technology.

FROM ONE CHALLENGE TO ANOTHER

The development and growth of any establishment is not easy. Al-Quds Paints Co. faced many challenges; and, aside from the normal difficulties, the factory faced severe financial, technical and manpower-skills concerns.

First challenge: 'it was hard to breathe normally'

Regarding the financial difficulties, Amer said: 'My father went to the bank and sold most of his personal stock in order to provide the minimum capital required. This made things worse, because the bank would not hold if we were not on time. It always felt as if we were being chased with a collector's bat. Furthermore, the funds provided only half of what we needed in terms of raw materials, machinery and running costs. Our ability to compete was undercut. For every Jordanian dinar (JD) of debt, JD10 of credit were needed soon. It was very hard to breathe normally.'

Second challenge: possessing chemical formulas does not ensure success

Possessing chemical formulas does not ensure success. Indeed, the staff needed technical experience in purchasing, storing, manufacturing, buying, managing, selling, quality control etc. 'The first batch we produced was supposed to be water-based putty. The product looked like a clam chowder soup – but not edible. We needed to learn the hard way something called "Chemical Sequenced Process",' Amer Said.

Third challenge: learning the hard way

To begin with, only Amer and his brother Samer worked in the factory. They would start mixing at 4 p.m. and finish at 1 a.m., just to produce one batch. Today it takes just 45 minutes to produce a batch. Then, Amer would load the product into his truck and take it to the market to sell. Three months later, they hired one worker to help Samer while Amer was in the market, selling. One year later, Maher, the third brother, joined them. Two years after that, they hired a part-time accountant.

They did not know how to deal with chemicals. They learned that lack of knowledge is dangerous in this kind of chemical industry. One day Amer took a sniff from a sealed plastic container of ammonia, and almost died of suffocation. That was the result of not having labelled the container to indicate that its contents were toxic.

Then father Jamil Jubran, who had invested all his savings and placed his possessions as collateral with the bank, decided to leave his sons on their own with this project. He gathered them in a meeting and told them that he trusted them to protect the family business, but advised them to work hard to strengthen it, and reminded them that nothing comes easily.

This was a tough start and a real challenge. 'We were focused on one thing: to produce a better-quality putty and cement-based tile adhesive than the rest of the market, yet to sell it at a lower price than our competitors, no matter what it took. Our total number of employees was five, including the owners and one part-time accountant. It was a very rough beginning, between the years 1994 and 2000, with very low sales, or even financial losses. The only bright spot during that period was the top quality of our putties and tile adhesive!' Amer said.

Eventually, the early lessons paid off.

GAINING A REPUTATION FOR QUALITY

Amer continued: 'By 2000, the Jordanian market was beginning to realise the consistency of the quality of Al-Quds Paints products. There was a slight increase in demand and more brand recognition. However, the product family was not expanding to include more, complementary products, such as paints. By the end of 2003, the total number of employees was 10, including one full-time sales co-ordinator and one full-time accountant. By then, almost all the loans had been paid off.'

To achieve Al-Quds Paints Co.'s objectives, Amer did his best to help and support the co-operative inquiry team to develop and transform the factory.

Undertaking the Co-operative Inquiry

THE FIRST REFLECTION PHASE: EXPLAINING I.THEORY

During the first year of my consulting assignment I took the opportunity to pursue a co-operative inquiry methodology, and participated in Al-Quds Paints Co. quality circles as one of the co-operative team. We held weekly meetings in which everyone was encouraged to express themselves and share their knowledge and experience on best practice. My role was to explain I.Theory and the practice of Islamic values in management, and their relation to quality and transformation. In addition, I led workshop sessions on TQM, set in the context of I.Theory in management, including on how to build HR systems. Most of the team focused on building up Al-Quds Paints Co.'s image by developing the company's vision and mission. In this context, we incorporated concepts of I.Theory in management.

All employees in the factory are Muslims. Maher thus follows Prophet Mohammad's policy at work: never to scold. 'One of Prophet Mohammad's workers said, "Never did the Prophet ask me why I did not do this, or why I did that." And the Prophet said, "Give your worker his wages before his sweat has dried."' (Saheeh Muslim)

THE FIRST ACTION PHASE: AL QUDS PAINTS VISION AND MISSION

During my meeting with the co-operative inquiry team, I asked them about their vision and mission. With the exception of Amer Jubran, the General Manager, no one knew what those expressions meant. I explained that vision pointed the way to the future (long term), and that according to it you should build programmes and plans. I felt their enthusiasm to have a clear vision and mission. After one month of discussions and exchange of ideas, they agreed upon the following:

> *Al Quds Vision: To place Al-Quds Paints Co. in the lead of water-based paint companies in Jordan and abroad, whereby the company's paints are used in every house, whereby the company is committed to high quality and reasonable prices.*

'How can their paints adorn every house?' I wondered.

> *Al Quds Mission: Al-Quds Paints Co. seeks to be known as one of the best producers of water-based paints in Jordan. With its reasonable prices, it seeks to attract the greatest number of customers from all economic levels, develop new products and expand into local and external markets, thereby increasing earnings for both investors and employees.*

For me, it was a great achievement and a cornerstone for our organisational development and, indeed, a transformation, come up with this. 'But what does transformation mean?' I asked during our meetings in March 2008.

Amer Jubran replied: 'Transformation means radical change in all aspects in our organisation. That's what I have been trying to do since 2004, when I took over the company's management. The company is transformed from a one-man show to specialised corporate departments such as financial, marketing, human resources, manufacturing etc.'

Haifa said: 'I believe in change, but we need a leader to guide the process; and we have our general manager who is making this change.'

Ola continued: 'There are transformational processes under way. The company hired me last year as quality assurance officer to be responsible for the lab and all paint testing, as a major step towards quality and transformation.'

Maher focused on Islamic values in the company, and said: 'If all workers and employees follow Islamic principles and values, I am sure that our company will be transformed to achieve the vision we have set.'

'What values are you talking about?' I asked. He said: 'Of course we have a lot of Islamic values such as *Amanah* (honesty), *Taqwa*, truthfulness, sincerity, faithfulness.'

Amer clarified other organisational values related to Islamic values and said: 'There are real values that I believe in, and make I sure they are followed, like teamwork, delegation of responsibility, accountability, sharing profits and accomplishment. However, the most important value of all is the collective contribution of thoughts and solutions (*Shura* and mutual consultation). This value leads to a real partnership between the owners/managers and the employees, which is a major contributor to the success of Al-Quds Paints Co. today.'

'But what about justice as an Islamic value?' I asked.

Maher said: 'We have adopted the justice value in our company by implementing performance evaluation. We keep records for each worker to document his strengths and weaknesses in order to reward him for his strengths and take actions to correct any errors. Also, we ensure that the path of justice is followed in wages and salaries in the company, and we try to be just in everything we do by adhering to what Allah says in the Qur'an: *"When you judge between men, judge with justice"'* (sura Al-Nisa, aya 58).

Samer added: 'Islam requires Muslims to be fair and act justly when documenting contracts. Another admirable example of justice is *Zakat* (alms), which is the poor's share in the wealth of the rich. The holy Qur'an made justice mandatory in everything in life, not only inside work.'

'Indeed, but how can you put these values into practice in your company?' I asked.

Maher said: 'We behave towards our workers with humility; I do not give orders. If a worker is sick, the company pays all the medical expenses, despite the fact that we do not have health insurance. And we pay our charity and our *Zakat* to our workers and employees. So the loyalty of our workers is very high. We share in their happiness and sadness, as if we were one family. For example, as an owner of and partner in the company, I started work in 1996 as a worker, carrying the materials on my back and putting them in the store. My vision was that we should succeed as a family business and gain some profits to develop our company and build our name in the market. I kept developing my work and have been the Production Manager since 2000. We were producing one kind of putty, called Silky Coat, in addition to some kinds of paint adhesives. But now we have many kinds of putty, such as water putties (three types: blade-application, spray and crack treatment); also we have finishing putties (such as velvet effect, stucco effect and pearly stucco effect), in addition to decorative paints such as plain white (four types) and tintable paints (10 types), and many kinds of adhesives. So our company has been transformed because we have implemented our Islamic values as a way of life.'

After an in-depth discussion with the co-operative inquiry team about values and transformation, and the values that we needed to agree upon to include in the company's charter, to be implemented by all employees and workers, we agreed upon the following as core values for the company:

- *Taqwa* – sense of responsibility and self-control
- Justice
- Co-operation.

As a co-researcher, I conducted a workshop for all workers and employees to explain these values and why we had included them in the company's charter. To have *Taqwa* means that everyone in the company should keep God in their sight while they work and know that while they cannot see Him, He can see them. This way, they will monitor their work by themselves and their sense of responsibility and accountability in all aspects, whether professional or personal, will increase, making the enforcement of a control policy unnecessary.

Justice, the core value of Islam, is adopted in building HR systems, as we saw in the RSCN case, such as wages and incentives.

As for the co-operation value, it is a major factor in creating team spirit. Many new products can be created through co-operation and the sharing of knowledge and experience among all workers and employees. I told them during the workshop: 'You should not compete among yourselves. You should compete in the market with your competitors.'

Furthermore, as a co-researcher and management consultant, I arranged many meetings to discuss the questionnaire on Heron's knowledge modes that I had distributed, which involved:

- Experiential knowledge
- Presentational knowledge
- Propositional knowledge
- Practical knowledge.

THE FIRST REFLECTION PHASE: THE KNOWLEDGE MODES

Experiential knowledge

The three brothers running Al-Quds Paints Co. have ample experience and knowledge between them. They established the factory together in 1996 and have some experienced employees; however, the majority of the workers and employees are more recently employed, following the company's growth.

I raised the question: 'How is your work developing?'

Amer, as General Manager, answered: 'Development is under way as planned. It can be measured in the huge change achieved since 2004, when I took over the company. The company was transformed from a one-man show into specialised corporate departments such as finance, marketing, HR, production etc., in addition to the currently implemented IT programs, such as Enterprise Resources Planning (ERP).'

Ola Atteiyeh answered the question from her point of view: 'My experience in Al-Quds Paints Co. is based on only one year as Quality Assurance Officer. During this year we have established a new lab with new equipment for testing; we achieved ISO 9001 and ISO 14001 certification; and the company has enhanced my knowledge base through my participation in and application of training courses in the technical and managerial areas. We will continue our development to open new markets, and we are looking for new products. We will develop a new research and development department. I have put all my knowledge of chemistry and chemical materials into developing Al-Quds Paints Co. We are one (the company and I), as you mentioned when you explained the Islamic Theory of management to us. I believe that I.Theory fosters unity between management or owners and all employees.'

Salem said: 'I have gained all my experience in the factory. I now know how I should arrange and classify the raw materials. I also know how to communicate and deal professionally with suppliers. I have gained much benefit during my work in Al-Quds Paints Co., such as warehousing experience, by attending training courses. I supervise two workers, with whom I share my knowledge. There is trust between us.'

Khaled tried to explain his unique experience in the maintenance department: 'I have gained a great deal of knowledge in this company because there are opportunities for the creation and innovation of new and good things. I started in the company as a maintenance supervisor. We then had sub-contractors performing maintenance duties. During my work in the maintenance department I found myself doing all the mechanical and electrical maintenance. I also designed the filters in the production hall as a requirement for ISO 14001.'

Ammar Abu Dawoud, Project Manager, is very optimistic about the development and growth of the company. He said: 'I had not heard about Al-Quds Paints Co. before my first interview with the General Manager, Mr Amer Jubran. I had one year of experience in a computer trading company and joined this company as the ERP Project Manager. I discovered that there was no ERP system in the company and I helped the General

Manager to select one. After we bought the system, I had a very important role, holding meetings to explain each process of system. To begin with, I had some difficulties with the workers and employees; but after a while, with the help of the General Manager, we were all co-operating closely.'

Haifa was a secretary before joining Al-Quds Paints Co. From the first day she felt the family atmosphere in the company. She drew on all her relevant experience and has been promoted to Administrative Assistant. In her new position, she has gained a lot of new knowledge because she wanted to know everything about IT, HR, production, procurement. After she had proved herself in these new areas, the General Manager promoted her to be the Local Procurement Manager. Haifa said: 'I tried to increase my knowledge through the internet, and strove to develop my skills, despite some opposition. All of our staff are experienced; we now have about 100 employees and three showrooms and outlets.'

Haifa said: 'The Islamic values that we believe in encourage the senior management and employees to be one unit; and that unification leads to continuous improvement. These are the two main concepts of the Islamic Theory in management.'

During our meetings with the co-operative inquiry team at Al-Quds Paints Co., I asked if they knew about international management approaches, such as the Western and Japanese approaches. Only Amer Jubran answered. 'Western management depends on individuals being productive, regardless of circumstances or past history. It focuses on control and measurement.' He went on to say: 'From my experience, the Western school of management depends on materialistic needs (profits) more than human ones. So-called social responsibility is a public relations feel-good type of effort and not a real value. However, some of the management sciences, such as financial management, HR management and production management etc. are very valuable if used with a proper set of core values.

'The Japanese school of management is more concerned with the quality of goods, process, materials etc. The focus on humans is built into models of otherwise rigid control that show an ideal condition, but underneath it is not so ideal. The set of values is almost a set of military orders, to be executed without challenge! However, the Japanese school of management produces better teamwork and better-quality products compared to the Western style of management.'

During one of my meetings, I explained the differences in values between Japanese and Western management styles, especially in the implementation of HR systems and how the Japanese achieved TQM with their value system, which is based on their egalitarian beliefs. In addition, I explained the elements of TQM that lead to a high quality of product, which can be seen in Japanese products all over the world.

Amer Jubran said: 'My first impression of TQM is that it does not function as a control system if the core of control does not believe in and is not armed with a good moral system. In Al-Quds Paints Co., our first priority was to establish a set of moral values, such as respect within the internal and external environments. This included quality of product and quality of conduct at all levels. I found that the best way to achieve this was by allowing the employees and the customers to participate in it; simply listening to them and learning from them.'

We then turned to a second reflection, on imaginal knowledge.

Imaginal knowledge

I now focused on the imaginal knowledge of each member of the co-operative inquiry team after they had agreed on their vision and mission, and on which strategies to incorporate with this vision and mission at work.

Izzeddeen Abu Zir, who is the Showroom Officer, told me that he used his vision and mission with each customer to create some kind of loyalty based on truth or *Amanah* in work as an Islamic value. He said: 'If a customer wants to buy red paint for his child's room, I advise him that painting the entire room red will encourage violence. Red should be used on only one wall or corner. If the customer is still determined to take red for all the walls and is not convinced, I urge him to sleep on my advice about the social effect of colours, and come back to buy the paint some other time.'

This was the first time I had heard about the psychological impact of colours on the behaviour of children, and how the idea is used in advising customers. Izzeddeen believes not only in selling high-quality paints but also in being honest with customers about colours and their effects.

I felt the honesty that the salespeople demonstrated when dealing with customers. For example, if a customer asked for a large quantity of paint or putty, they would ask for how many square metres the paint was needed and advise him or her to buy only the necessary quantity. They were looking not only to make a profit, but also to be honest with their customers.

Maher Jubran said: 'My point of view as Production Manager, regarding imaginal knowledge, is this: We have embarked on this transformation journey in our factory. I try to learn and to develop myself so as to accumulate knowledge in all the fields related to my work, and to use the pyramids of knowledge to share the basic data, information, knowledge and wisdom with my colleagues. In addition, I use planning in my work because I have learned that we should think of both the present and the future, as God ordered us in the Qur'an.'

Amer Jubran said: 'We must capitalise on opportunities and turn them into reality. For example, a plan was organised around a goal that was to be achieved, and how to execute and implement the steps needed to bring about the change. However, willingness to change on the part of the owners and employees was very helpful in ensuring the success of the plan, because all took part in the decision-making and planning process. My philosophy for transformation at Al-Quds Paints is focused on:

1. 'Generating a discussion among the partners themselves, the partners and key persons in the company, and among the key persons and the rest of the employees.
2. 'Documenting rules of conduct for both professional and personal behaviours, based on the ideas arrived at in phase one.
3. 'Gradual implementation, to ensure comprehension and conviction.
4. 'Auditing and control through the joint efforts of partners, key personnel and employees, to ensure implementation.

'I integrate all the Islamic values, such as *Shura*, *Taqwa* and justice, in these sequential stages, in addition to decentralisation and team co-operation. Without losing sight of the fact that my company is a profit-making establishment, I want it to be built on a sound, ethical base by everyone involved, and at all levels. On the other hand, I have built my organisation to be a learning environment by encouraging learning and raising the competencies of our workers through managerial and technical training.'

Everyone in the co-operative inquiry team agreed with Amer. In fact everyone had participated in at least five different external workshops in 2008 and 2009, not to mention internal learning meetings, which reflected positively on their relationships with each other and between employees and senior management and owners. The learning sessions involved the participation of employees in decision making, especially in the production department, to improve quality or suggest ideas for continuous improvement. After more than a year's implementation of the values in which senior management believed, they were announced in the company's charter, to enable employees to better envisage their future.

'Let us see the impact of Islamic values on the employees,' I said.

Amer Jubran answered my question and said: 'The impact is very clear:

- 'The consensus policy we used during our meetings
- 'Commitment to act without double standards or favouritism
- 'Providing means of resolving conflicts such as forming committees and delegating authorities.

'In addition, we are focusing on time management (making sure it is fair to all), better quality and ensuring everyone's commitment to our code of ethics, which we put into our charter. As to co-operative and participatory action in the company, we encourage creative thinking, divide responsibility so as to reduce risks and give benefits to all our employees in the form of profit sharing.

'Our systems are based on the Islamic Theory of management. For example, the selection and recruitment system is based on strength and honesty.

'Strength means physical fitness, sociological fitness and professional fitness. Honesty means values, logic and methodology. The performance appraisal system includes positive and negative points in the following four categories:

1. General system
2. Efficiency
3. Relationship
4. Continuous improvement.

This evaluation will be implemented on a continuous basis. Positive and negative points are to be recorded for the final evaluation and included in the incentives system.'

Maher Jubran added: 'We focus on the truth value in addition to the values in our charter. If any worker or employee is not telling the truth, we discuss the matter with him, separately, until he admits his wrong behaviour; if not, he will be punished according to the penalty system. Also, we give our employees an extra 16 days on top of their official annual leave, as an incentive, which makes them happy in their work.'

We now turn from experiencing the past and present and imagining the future, to linking the two through organisational cultural and strategic concepts.

SECOND ACTION PHASE: BUILDING CULTURAL SYSTEMS

Conceptual knowledge

When I got the consulting assignment with Al-Quds Paints Co. to build the HR systems, early in 2008, I was eager to start implementing the I.Theory of management and to build an organisational culture based on a values-managed organisation. Amer Jubran, as the General Manager, gave me the green light for this development process, which took about one year with commitment from the top management.

First of all, I formed my co-operative inquiry team, as mentioned at the beginning of the chapter, and started many workshops to integrate Islamic values into their work.

The first workshop was about the importance of work and how it is a form of worship. I told the participants the story about some people who asked Prophet Mohammad about their friend, who spent all day and night praying. The Prophet asked them: *'Who gives him to eat and drink?'* They said that they did, so the Prophet said: *'You are better than him.'* This means that to worship is not only to pray day and night; God ordered us to work and lead good lives as well.

Prophet Mohammad also said: *'Never has anyone eaten a food better than that earned by his hands.'* But Islam does not see working for worldly gain only as sufficient; it requires also the touch of worship and devotion to God.

I focused on the employees' contracts with the company and insisted that they should be based on honesty. If people do not give their time to work as they should, it means that they are not being honest with God, themselves and the organisation. So workers and employees should work as if God can see them and is recording both the positive and the negative things they are doing. Also, management should give employees all their rights in order to meet their objectives. In such circumstances we will see unity between staff and senior management.

Two months after this workshop, Maher Jubran, the Production Manager, asked me: 'What have you done with our workers? They have changed their behaviour in the factory.' I asked him: 'How?' He said: 'The one-hour lunch and prayer breaks at midday were a problem, because they usually leave their machines for the break and don't return on time, which leads to wasted time. But now they are returning on time on their own, without me having to remind them.' I appreciated their new attitude of behaving according to their beliefs and not just according to working hours.

The second session I conducted was about the vision and mission of Al-Quds Paints Co., including the charter that we had devised with the co-operative inquiry team. I explained the meaning of vision and mission, and how the employees, as workers, should implement them by doing their work right, from the start, and every time. This was another point the company could consider and achieve in the long-term. It was not a dream. It was a strategic choice for the company to put all its resources and efforts into, so as to grasp and achieve it.

The company's vision states that Al-Quds Paints Co. is to become a leader both within and outside Jordan, and to become a part of each and every household. This vision exerts pressure on the company to produce high-quality products, sold at reasonable prices. It is therefore necessary to save time, costs and re-working of batches, in addition to controlling and testing all products in the lab. Through such an attitude to the work, it will achieve its vision.

As for the mission, I explained to all the workers what it meant:

- Why was the company established?
- What values are followed?
- What is the core value followed in internal relationships and external relationships?
- In which market are we working?
- Which customers are we serving?
- Motivated and aspiring.
- Workable and achievable.
- Convincing and trustworthy.

So they knew what products were produced, for which market, with what kind of quality and for what price. But why should they develop their products and be keen for the company's growth? The answer was very easy: so that they could increase their income and earnings. The owner, the Jubran family, was committed to sharing the benefits so as to increase the workers' income and give wages and incentives based on their work, and according to just and fair practices. Moreover, they should commit themselves to the following:

1. Building a strong relationship with customers, and working with them as one team through their good-quality products.
2. Developing their competencies.
3. Encouraging good performance and creative thinking.
4. Encouraging teamwork and team spirit.
5. Being committed to the company's objectives, and developing the skills of all staff members.
6. Taking the opportunity for development and research, especially with the newly equipped lab.
7. Trying to maintain and preserve the environment from pollution.
8. Trying to maintain quality, according to the highest standards.

Now for the values.

If the staff complied with these requirements, they would achieve their mission, through committed human resources and their Islamic values. These values underlay how they worked and conducted themselves:

> *Taqwa*: It is a way of life and work in corporations. It means each employee should behave towards himself, his supervisors, his subordinates, his instruments and tools and the owners with the realisation that faith in God is the standard for behaviour. So one should behave with self-control, not police control.

> *Justice*: It is the basic value. It is an ultimate value for any society, organisation and life in general. With justice in HR systems implementation, employee satisfaction, transparency and accountability will be ensured.

Co-operation: This is a power driver among all human resources inside the company, not competition or conflict. Co-operation is a power for innovation and creation in any organisation and the means for achieving its vision and mission.

The top management and the co-operative inquiry team had agreed upon the company's charter, which was to be read and implemented. The charter reflected the values system, which called for a high level of commitment to work and saw the company as a single unit (the staff and senior management together). The oath that employees take exemplifies this:

a)   I will do my best.
b)   I will be careful.
c)   I will work only for my company.
d)   I will maintain confidentiality.
e)   I will report any harm to my company etc.

The third workshop was held one month later, to work my way through the HR systems that we had agreed upon with the co-operative inquiry team and that had been signed off by the General Manager, Amer Jubran. These systems covered the following:

1.   Selection and recruitment: based on strength and honesty, with all their standards and forms.
2.   Pyramidal structuring and gradation scale, with I.Theory confirming that variation in employment does not necessarily mean social variation and does not affect the spirit of social equality.
3.   Promotion: based on faith and knowledge. In this regard, the Qur'an exalts and raises the grades of people with faith and values who continue to learn and seek new knowledge. I encouraged workers to read and to develop themselves in order to develop their company.
4.   Performance appraisal: based on online records of th bothe positive and negative actions of each employee. Evaluations and pay raises are based on these appraisals. The justice value is very clear in this evaluation system because the reward is based on each employee's appraisal.
5.   Wages and salaries: the top management agreed upon a salary scale that guarantees justice and is based on position, experience, education and skills.
6.   Incentives: focused on satisfaction, not fulfilment, and on group motivation, in addition to individual motivation. People should work as one team to achieve their own objectives and the company's objectives.
7.   Training assessment needs and training plan: from time to time everyone will have opportunities for continuous learning to increase their knowledge and skills. The top management is committed to raising staff competencies. This will lead Al-Quds Paints Co. to continuous improvement.

During these workshops and other meetings, I tried to build a new culture on the ground to help workers to accept the new atmosphere in the factory. One of them told me: 'If we practise systems and work and behave as God asked us to do, I am sure that the company will grow and develop and will achieve its vision and mission.'

I replied: 'I will come back after six months to test progress in all aspects of the company.'

But why and how did we build systems in Al-Quds Paints Co.?

STRATEGIC GROWTH

Prior lack of vision

In early 2004, Amer Jubran had provided his partners with an analytical critique of the company. The most important thing about which they agreed was that the company did not have a vision or plan for either the short or the long term. They agreed to establish two goals: first, revive the goals that they had when they started the company. Second, make a plan of three stages: short, medium and long term. The short-term plan focused on increasing the market share of their products. They succeeded in promoting awareness of their brands. The medium-term plan focused on expanding the product range to include paints and decorative paints, and this depended on their trade affiliation with big European raw materials suppliers who had strong research and development (R&D) facilities. The long-term plan aimed to build an organisation with a full HR cadre who were to be partners in creating success.

In 2005, the company added the following to its line of water-based products:

- four brands of emulsion paints
- three brands of decorative emulsions
- ten brands of decorative paints.

The market's acceptance of the products was very promising because quality and competitive pricing continued to be the governing policy.

Company's development projects

During 2007, the company completed a full diagnostic study to upgrade its capacity and capability. It was working on carrying out a plan to develop the following:

- Get ISO 9001 and ISO 14001 certification with TEAM. It was certified during 2008, so it built the Quality Management System as a first step to building capability in the company.
- Start a chain of colour tinting centres, using modern European tinting systems.
- Build a modern laboratory to accommodate both quality control and R&D needs.

In addition, it implemented a strategy of developing the leadership capabilities and skills of its young and enthusiastic working team. Intensive training programmes were attended by all departments.

In early 2008, Amer Jubran asked me at TEAM International to build the human resources systems and to create a new culture in his company. I understood his vision for growth and development, especially to expand the market to cover the region, North Africa and Europe. The partners understood that this was a serious challenge, and they were willing to accept it.

The transformation journey

After they had understood what transformation meant, I started with the co-operative inquiry team to build the company's organisational structure (OS), which reflected all the activities and, most importantly, the new activity of the Quality Assurance department. The OS gives each activity the position needed, regardless of the departments, sections or units. Each member of the co-operative team was responsible for documenting on the OS the steps of their work in every unit. We then reviewed it together and issued the OS manual for the units' specifications.

The second manual issued was the Employee Manual, covering the following:

- Vision, mission, values and company charter
- Company regulations and work instructions with all necessary forms.

How did we formulate the vision, mission and values?

As a consulting assignment, I arranged for a weekly meeting with the co-operative inquiry team so as to build the new manuals and systems with their participation. The first meetings, to set the vision and mission, were very difficult because I suggested a vision for them, as a small company, to keep their quality as it was and expand into regional markets.

Amer said: 'No, our vision will be to be a leader not only in the local market, but abroad, in any market we can access.' I said: 'But we have giant paints companies in Jordan such as National, Dulux, and so on. Also, these companies have brand names and some of them are producing under licence.'

He insisted that we develop a vision by which we should start to access new markets. He went to the United Arab Emirates to arrange for exports.

Samer said: 'We should enter each house that needs paints in Jordan and implement our vision, keeping in mind quality of the highest order and selling our products at reasonable prices. We will start with a promotional campaign.'

Finally all of the co-operative inquiry team agreed on the vision:

> To place Al-Quds Paints Company in the lead of water-based paints companies in Jordan and abroad, to be part of the paints supplements in every house, and be committed to high quality and reasonable prices.

The mission, for its part, reflected the vision of producing high-quality water-based paints and increasing market share. The team committed themselves to developing new products and accessing markets abroad. Their objective was to increase profits for both investors and employees.

I asked them: 'How can we achieve that? We should believe in our capabilities, follow our Islamic values such as *Itqan* (quality of work), and let work be a form of worship. So we should increase our values.'

I started with the first value: *Taqwa*. Every one of the co-operative inquiry team members looked at me with surprise. 'How can we put *Taqwa* into our mission?' one of them asked me. 'Is it necessary to announce to people that we have *Taqwa* in the values we that issue and commit to?'

Maher said: 'Of course we should announce that to everybody, for our credibility and so as to gain the trust of the public. We also need *Taqwa* within each one of us in order to control our work and do it with *Itqan*.'

Amer asked: 'Do we need to explain *Taqwa* in our mission?' He answered himself: 'I do not think so, because the meaning of *Taqwa* is very clear, so we should put *Taqwa* as a sense of responsibility.'

Next came justice. I explained the meaning of justice generally, and in Islam specifically. Justice is an independent value. It is easy to practise in our systems. All the staff would feel comfortable. With justice, we would have transparency in all elements or systems. We cannot say that we have half justice, or some percentage of it. The senior management must implement justice in all systems. Evaluation, incentives, any award given to anyone should be based on very clear elements.

Haifa asked: 'How can we practise justice in Al-Quds Paints Co.? It is something related to senior management only, because they have the authority to apply justice, and it is according to their point of view.'

Izzeddeen Abu Zir commented: 'From my point of view as a supervisor of all the employees in the showrooms, I need very clear attributes to be able to implement and practise this great value in our work.'

'Justice is the first value in the Islamic course, and we will build our systems accordingly. Also, we should do our work with justice, for example when we build the salary scale, incentives system and evaluation appraisal system. Even our behaviour with subordinates should be done with justice,' I said.

Co-operation, the third value, should be added as an Islamic value. God ordered us to practise co-operation in our lives in order to have a good life and achieve quality of life. The importance of co-operation was that it would lead to creation and innovation inside the company. It would also create team spirit and teamwork. Finally, we could see the unification or alignment inside Al-Quds Paints Co. within the co-operative inquiry team, and between all the staff and the senior management.

All members of the co-operative inquiry team agreed to this, and I asked them to give me examples of co-operation amongst them.

Ola said: 'For me as Quality Assurance Officer, I feel the co-operation everyday with my colleagues in the company, especially during the implementation stage of the quality management system and after we got the ISO 9001:2008 certification. All the staff are keen to practise and implement the documentation of quality, such as forms or records. When we had the audit visit from the certification body, the auditor saw how we were committed to implementation of the QMS system. So if we did not have that kind of co-operation, we could not have achieved our goal.'

Haifa continued: 'If I have a lot of work, many colleagues offer their help, and I can finish my work with their co-operation. On the other hand, if I need more knowledge on any subject, I seek it from others.'

Izzeddeen Abu Zir said: 'For me the value of co-operation is like a football team, which has a goal keeper, an attack team, a defence team, and a mid-field team. They work together as one team. If the goal keeper loses, the whole team will lose. If anyone works in a good way, the result is not only for him but for the whole team.

'We are working as a team in Al-Quds Paints Co. because we all have the same interests. For example, in March 2008 one of the showrooms had an order for a large quantity of coloured paints to be delivered in a short time. All the other employees in the other showrooms helped and supported them to produce the required quantity on time. The point here is that the action was self-initiated. It was not an order from the top management.'

Now that Al-Quds Paints Co. accepted and pursued the meaning of values, it became easy to formulate the charter in the next meeting. We now turn to the charter.

Al-Quds charter

The charter of Al-Quds Paints Co. includes the vision, mission and values as mentioned above, in addition to the oath. The oath is as follows:

As I am a member of the Al-Quds Paints Co. family and believe in its vision, mission and values, I swear that:

1. *I will be an effective and productive member.*

2. *I will do my best to stop any maltreatment of any co-worker.*

3. *I will resist in myself any envy or hatred.*

4. *I will not spy on any co-worker.*

5. *I will co-operate with all co-workers, and will not be in conflict with any of them.*

6. *I will keep and maintain all machines or equipment in a good shape.*

7. *I will maintain secrecy and company confidentiality, even after I leave the company.*

8. *I will give all my mental and professional efforts to achieving the company's objectives and employee's objectives.*

9. *I will tell the top management about any wrong action that happens, so as to take corrective or preventive actions.*

10. *I will respect others.*

11. *I will take responsibility for my words and work.*

12. *I will protect the credibility and reputation of the company.*

13. *I will commit myself to abiding by the company's regulations and work instructions.*

To begin with, reaction to this oath was not as expected; but after I had given another lecture, the workers began to believe in it and to implement it.

Two weeks later, during our weekly meetings, I started to build the HR systems with the co-operative inquiry team members. We discussed them, then put them into practice.

I gave the factors for systems such as selection and recruitment, career path, promotion, salary scale, incentives, performance appraisal, needs assessment, human resources planning and the human resources auditing; and the team modified these according to the needs of Al-Quds Paints Co.

My focus was on the new concept of performance appraisal as an online performance evaluation, with new forms. It was based on a special register to record the positive or negative actions of each employee. The line manager would perform it.

What I noticed in Al-Quds Paints Co. was that the basic salaries were above the minimum official rate the Ministry of Labour in Jordan, as set out in the Labour Law. The philosophy of senior management is to give people what is equal to their efforts. After six months, I returned to Al-Quds Paints Co. to see whether it had completed the checklist of the auditing system, and also to see the evidence of the new practices.

FINAL REFLECTION PHASE: MONITORING AND EVALUATION

The transformation under way

With the transformation process under way at Al-Quds Paints Co., I monitored the feedback on the process and how the company was changing.

Amer Jubran, as General Manger, was running his company in a way that ensured smooth growth and a good position in the local market. He intended to develop the personnel to become more competent and made sure that everybody felt respected and was making a better living than before.

'The important thing that is helping the company to change is the Islamic values. They are a reason for our success, but need to be measured using successful financial and managerial models,' Amer Said.

As for the practical side, Amer said: 'This requires teamwork with a decisive and clear vision. Selection needs to be built on team members and group players.'

Izzeddeen added: 'In Al-Quds Paints Co. we practise all the systems that we have built together. For example, I feel that I am more than a partner because of the incentive system. I have had many opportunities to develop myself; and the senior management appreciates my efforts, morally and materially. If I receive only money for my work, that means I am like a machine; but if I have moral appreciation, I feel like one of the family. I feel social security inside my company, which I sometimes miss at home.

'I can say that I have changed 100%, especially mentally; and this change has affected the relationship between me and the senior management.'

Maher Jubran ensured that the Islamic values practices were applied on the ground. He gave an example of *Amanah* (honesty): 'One day, one of the workers made a mistake in the production. He came and confessed that it was his mistake and said he should pay the cost because it was his responsibility.'

From theory to action

After building of the systems and implementation of the transformation process, people felt that this radical change had led to an increase in productivity, which created a need to hire more employees. They recruited another 20 employees and workers in 2009, and implemented the selection and recruitment system for all the newcomers. The newcomers were introduced to the new environment in the company; they understood the vision and mission, signed the company charter and knew all the systems such as the salary scale, performance appraisal, training, incentives and so on.

I interviewed one of these newcomers, Ammar Abu Daoud. He holds a master's degree in Computer Information Systems. He was employed at Al-Quds Paints Co. as a Project Manager in early 2009. He felt the difference in atmosphere between this company and his previous company, where he could not meet his manager, but only received orders. 'What I have found here is another story. People are committed to work as if it were worship. They look for quality in everything. The managers (the Jubran brothers) are very committed and very humble with the employees; something I never experienced in my previous work,' Ammar said.

'What about the systems you found in Al-Quds Paints Co.?' I asked him. He said: 'First of all, I saw the HR Manager and he gave me the employees' manual, with all the regulations and work instructions, to read. I signed the charter and know the vision and mission of the company. I received my job description, according to which I should take the technical projects in the company and start my work. My relationship is directly with Amer, the General Manager. I feel that I am with a new family. We all like each other. If any part of this body is unwell, all of us will be affected. This is the difference. Also, I have seen all the documented procedures for each activity because Al-Quds Paints Co. is ISO 9001 certificated; so this is another difference from other companies.'

'What about the company's objectives and your objectives within the company?' I asked.

He said: 'There is no difference between them because the company's objectives are also mine; and Amer informed me that if I succeed in my work, I will share in the company's success. In addition, I like the fact that the culture of all employees is based on our Islamic values.'

Resistance to change

1. The most important thing facing the transformation journey is the inevitable resistance to change from some staff members. This affects the whole process negatively. Some people behave with selfishness, and without a code of ethics.
2. Insufficient financial resources to complete all the development processes.
3. Inadequate infrastructure in the factory.
4. The transformation process from family business to institutional organisation: accountability, transparency and delegation are not so easily achieved because of centralised management. The General Manager is used to being involved in everything in a centralised style of management.

Future steps

I met the co-operative inquiry team to draw up our future steps after we had finished building and implementing the systems.

Ola Attiyeh, the Quality Assurance Manager, who was also assigned to R&D, said: 'The market needs new products, so I should play a new role with the Production Manager to develop new putty and paint products. The weak point in our factory is the old machines, and we are looking forward to developing and improving them. Also, the types of raw material that we buy from external suppliers should be improved and have better specifications in order for us to be able to produce new products and always be in front.'

Amer, the General Manager, said: 'I look for our dynamic company to make continuous progress and development. This needs a strategic plan and a follow-up system to achieve the following:

1.   'Successful branding, while maintaining our high quality, reasonable prices and good services, and
2.   'Employees who feel at ease and are not overworked.'

I asked: 'What about your social responsibility in the company? How do you translate it as an Islamic concept and put it on the road map of your company's development, especially now that you have achieved the ISO 14001 certification, which covers the environmental management system?'

Amer continued: 'Of course, for our social responsibility role, we have already started the following:

1.   'Produce environmentally friendly products (lead free and mercury free, with low or no volatile organic compounds).
2.   'Start a strong link with students from Jordanian universities to prepare their research with our R&D department; in this case both sides will benefit.
3.   'Look into creating jobs for new graduates to give them an opportunity to start work and gain experience.'

Testing and validation

After one year, I went back to Al-Quds Paints Co. to see the results, and to see whether the Islamic culture was still there. I also wanted to see what positive outcomes had been achieved and if the company had faced any problems.

My first question to Amer was about the total revenue and the average change. He said: 'We have achieved a paradigm shift in revenues last year (2009) compared with 2008. We have also increased our staff according to the following table:

Table 11.1   Total revenue and staff during 2007–9

Year	Revenue (JD)	No. of employees
2007	2200000.000	40
2008	2500000.000	65
2009	3600000.000	85

Source: Al-Quds Paints Co. Management

'This means that the average change between 2009 and 2008 in revenues is 44 per cent, and the average change in staff between 2009 and 2008 is 30 per cent. This is reflected positively on the company's net profit.

'The incentives distributed among employees have been increased accordingly; the company's policy is to distribute 20 per cent of the net profit annually among all employees and workers, based on the performance appraisal system and its four dimensions (general system, efficiency and effectiveness, relationships: internal and external, and continuous improvement). In addition, the senior management decided to provide lunch and transport for the workers and employees.'

Production and technical systems transformation

The idea started when Amer Jubran recognised a clear weakness in his organisation's ability to meet customers' demands on time. He found out that the Al-Quds Paints Co. production department was always in a bottleneck. Then the question was raised: 'Is the mess in production and the warehouses a real problem or a symptom?'

Improvement of capacity has always been a concern for Amer, and the solution was either to: 1) make a big investment in new machines in order to increase the production rate, or 2) improve production planning, capacity planning, productivity, facility layout and applications integration.

So the mess looked like a symptom, and new machines could only increase the number of units produced without solving the real problem, and of course it would require an increase in resource allocation to operate the new machines properly.

Then Amer decided to proceed with the second solution. But where to start? Here he applied another Islamic value, *Shura* or consultation. He consulted with a specialised industrial consultant about what to do and where to start in order to solve the problems of production planning and integration.

The industrial consultant found that applications integration, or what is known as an Enterprise Resource Planning (ERP) system, would be the best way of improving the technical and production systems at Al-Quds Paints Co. The industrial consultant is also committed to Islamic values. In order to build effective production systems, two main Islamic values should be applied, *Itqan* and justice. As the consultant said: 'It is unfair to introduce the employees, who have never practised production planning, to an advanced ERP system without building a solid base and knowledge in order for them to understand and practise these systems before changing over to a computer-based production system. A computerised system is not a miracle, and to achieve *Itqan* all of the technical operators and employees need to understand every single detail, process, form and report of the technical and production system before applying them under a computerised environment.'

After careful consultation with the industrial consultant, Amer decided to start building the production system in the field; and with help from the industrial consultant Al-Quds Paints Co. started to build and implement the following systems:

- Demand Forecasting System
- Aggregate Planning System
- Master Production Scheduling (MPS) System
- Materials Requirements Planning (MRP) System

- Capacity Requirements Planning (CRP) System
- Bill of Materials (BOM)
- Computerised Maintenance Management System (CMMS)
- Layout Design and Warehouse Management System (WMS)

Upon completion and implementation of these systems, the ground was ready for the launch of the ERP project. The selection process for suitable ERP software took nearly a year and a half. Amer and the consultancy group met about 10 companies (local and regional). The final decision depended on transparency, justice and accurate performance (*Itqan*).

The implementation of ERP in Al-Quds Paints Co. was a difficult task, starting with the introduction of new concepts, going through training and culture change and ending with testing and validation of the system.

Technically, the ERP system has had a great effect on the company. It provides Al-Quds Paints Co. with online updates, reports, tracking, order processing, monitoring and control of each transaction, from the receipt of raw materials until delivery to customers/distributors and receipt of payments. The system results in better control, fewer mistakes, higher productivity and better customer satisfaction.

The ERP system has also had a cultural impact on Al-Quds Paints Co. This accurate, fast, reliable and cost-effective system teaches the users (Al-Quds Paints employees) to be ethical in their daily transactions. Several Islamic values were emphasised by the implementation of this applications integration (ERP) system. Basically, the ERP system emphasises *Itqan*, *Amanah*, justice and *Shura* as Islamic values at Al-Quds Paints Co.

Export markets

The company's strategic plan is based on its vision for opening new markets abroad, so it started to export putties and paints to the United Arab Emirates, Lebanon, Iraq and Egypt; but this was still a small percentage of the total production (only about 5% for the year 2009). It plans to increase the percentage of exports, especially now that it has many kinds of putties and paints, in addition to the environmentally friendly products.

Company market share

With the international financial crisis and its impact on Jordan in 2008–9, the market size is generally on the decrease, but the company's market share had remained the same. That means that the company has a high market share and high-quality products.

During the past two years, the company has made progress with its name Al-Quds Paints and the trade names of some putties, such as Silky Coat putty and QP tile adhesive. These two kinds are the best-known in Jordan and in the region, because of quality and demand. Also, demand has increased for the water-based paints, so the company had started to produce the environmentally friendly lines.

Action plan

There is no defined action plan as yet, but there are guidelines for what should be done as an action plan for the next three years:

- Develop Al-Quds Paints technology (products, machines and production lines).
- Develop the products towards international standards and international markets.
- Continuous development of HR: culturally, technically and morally.
- Al-Quds Paints now has very well-established systems, and has implemented and developed them based on the new issues in the company. Also, it is in the process of transforming the company into a learning organisation, technically and managerially.
- Meld the staff into one organisational team with the company's special spirit and image.
- Complete the Management Information System and ERP system to cover all the company's activities.

I will now turn to the conclusion of this long journey in quality and organisational transformation, and to the implications for future implementation.

Conclusions

Conclusions

CHAPTER 12 *Quality and Transformation: I.Theory Re-visited*

Introduction

THE JOURNEY I HAVE TAKEN

I am now coming to the end of my journey, in which I have taken my consulting company and my society, Jordan, with me through a composite co-operative inquiry into quality and transformation from a local–global perspective, using I.Theory as my vehicle. In the process, two major institutions in Jordan, one civic (RSCN) and the other industrial (Al-Quds Paints Co.), have been transformed, both reaching simultaneously into their past and their future. Inevitably, as a result, my own consulting practice is much more integral than it was before.

There are many books about Islam and Islamic thought, written by thinkers from around the Muslim world. They are divided into the following categories:

1. Books interpreting and explaining Qur'an or Sunnah.
2. Traditional philosophy books about existence and the unseen world.
3. Specific studies related to regulations in Islam focused on the individual human phenomenon and human rights, such as marriage, crimes, heritage, or on the collective human phenomenon and its goals.

Very few, if any, of these focus on the world of enterprise, whether public, private, civic or environmental. In this book I have done just that, focusing on quality and transformation from an Islamic perspective in both theory and, ultimately, practice. In the process of my informative and transformative, co-operative inquiry I have drawn upon 'scientific' method with a difference, not the usual so-called 'objective' and empirical method, but a more 'inter-subjective' and scientific approach.

THE ABSENCE OF JUSTICE IN THE WORLD

While I have been engaged in my journey – which in fact can be traced back to the 1960s and 1970s, starting out in Yemen – humanity has been in crisis (as Yemen is now) and massive injustice has prevailed at both the global and local levels. Powerful countries pressure weak countries through wars, occupation and the exploitation of wealth and resources to serve their own interests. Powerful dictators, moreover, within these weak countries, prevail upon their populations, powered by self-interest and all too oblivious of the needs of their people. In response to both of these injustices, we are today seeing an 'Arab Awakening', and I see my own work as integral to this.

The actions we are witnessing on the streets of Tunisia, Egypt and Libya, of Syria, Bahrain and Yemen, represent more or less successful attempts at democratisation, the pursuit of freedom, or rescue from oppressive or despotic systems. However, in no case yet, on an overall political or economic level, are we seeing explicit attempts to synthesise tradition and modernity, the local and the global – in my own case, Islamic wisdom with contemporary management thought.

Historically speaking, moreover, we have witnessed important developments in Western societies, such as the European Renaissance and Enlightenment, which were both revolutions against oppressive authorities and security systems, and a revisiting and renewal (Renaissance) of the classical past . We need something analogous to this in our own Arab Awakening.

Yet the philosophy of freedom followed by Western societies stands in the way of justice, in some respects, and has become the ultimate value, most especially in the economic realm, where 'free markets' and injustice go hand in hand (witness the latest financial crash, and its drastic effect on many parts of the world). This freedom often serves the elite in Western societies – if not elsewhere in the world – or their representatives, in the name of democracy. Nevertheless, the image of freedom on the Arab street, reinforced by access to social networks such as Facebook and Twitter – for young people largely modelled on 'Western' democracy – crowds out the picture of justice that I have painted here.

So what overall role does I.Theory have to play in this context?

I.Theory: Islamic, Itqan, International

I.Theory has been evolved, by Dr Assaf and me, as a management philosophy that is simultaneously Islamic and international. In other words, the focus on justice is by no means unique to Islam: it is just that in the Muslim world it has taken on particular prominence. 'I' stands for Islam, *Itqan* and International; it is for all people, in any place or time. It is the just complement and counterpart of freedom and equality: to bring people from conflict to co-operation, from hatred to love and from conflict to unity under the core value of *Taqwa* (God-revering behaviour).

The significance of *Taqwa*, for RSCN's Managing Director, is that of having a sense of responsibility in everything (Khaled, 2006):

- a sense of responsibility for individual actions toward others (International)
- a sense of responsibility for group destiny (Islam)
- a sense of responsibility for the continuous development of self, organisation and society (*Itqan*).

This, then, is not only for Islam or for Muslims, but for everyone in the world who is seeking to achieve his/her objectives by achieving the ultimate core values of the human phenomenon. In fact, and further to my own work on I.Theory, we would welcome further thoughts and actions from other faith affiliations on the role of justice in reformulating the practice of management, both locally and globally.

This places a huge responsibility on scholars, religious leaders and intellectuals to understand and reflect on Islam, if not also on Judaism and Christianity, Buddhism and Hinduism, as well as indigenous belief systems, so as to identify and embrace these values of justice in a management context. Sardar believes that this is possible 'only if we can operationalize its dynamic and vibrant concepts in contemporary society'. If we can do that, we can conceive and create social, economic and political orders for a Muslim civilisation of the future (Sardar, 1987). To enhance that, we also need foundations (Sardar, 2006) for the reconstruction of the Muslim civilisation so as to provide a knowledge base that can carry it forward and achieve well-being.

This focuses, moreover, on the quality of performance, ethically and spiritually, enhances the value of work as worship and, by implication, work as vocation. Here we need to renew our Islamic beliefs in contemporary terms. To the extent that Islam, and any other religion, places a primary value on justice, how can this be depicted in secular terms? For example, for Al-Jabri, a contemporary Moroccan Islamic philosopher (Al-Jabri, 1999), it is one thing to think through a tradition that has known continuous evolution into the present, a tradition that has been continuously renewed, revised and critiqued; and it is another thing to think through a tradition whose evolution was interrupted centuries ago, a tradition that is removed from the present by the deep gap that progress and science have dug between it and the present. I believe that I.Theory represents the former, rather than the latter.

As such, three steps must be taken, according to Sardar (2003):

1. Islam must be seen as an ethical framework, as a way of knowing, doing and believing.
2. Shariah or Islamic law must be seen its historic context and not elevated to the divine – it must be seen as an interpretive methodology for solving contemporary problems.
3. Muslims must become active seekers of the truth, and not passive recipients.

If these steps are taken, Islam can play a role in creating a global *Ummah* – a community of justice and a dynamic, thriving civilisation. In relation to this, at present, and in Jordan specifically, I am trying to introduce the concept of quality and transformation into organisations through my now newly integral consultancy work. I have to take into consideration, as a current reality, 'neo-patriarchal' Arab and Muslim managerial practices, which are both dependent on the Western managerial paradigm, and also all too often retrogressive 'pseudo-Islamic' beliefs. It is difficult to achieve the desired fusion between West, East and 'centre', so to speak, without an imaginative and systematic approach towards institutionalising the desired Arab and Muslim managerial paradigm based on Islamic values (I.Theory).

In general, we need an intellectual renaissance to accompany the socio-political Arab Awakening, a synthesis of moral and universal inspiration to rebuild civilisation and happiness–well-being. So what can we conclude about I.Theory in management, more specifically?

I.Theory in Management and Society

I have explained, throughout the course of this book, that I.Theory in management goes well beyond TQM because it consists of the following:

1. Unified objectives between individuals and groups: *Tawheed* (oneness).
2. Unified objectives of workers or employees, management or owners and society.
3. Basis on the effectiveness value, which means efficiency plus unification of objectives and continual improvement.
4. Basis on continual improvement through initiative, innovation and creation.
5. Incorporation of *Taqwa* in life, justice in enterprise, as well as freedom and equality.
6. Reflection of the justice orientation in any business or organisation through the implementation of HR systems according to I.Theory attributes.
7. Justice orientation that serves to promote balance in the community.
8. I.Theory focus on management by values; Islamic values thereby cover all aspects of life: social, political, economic and environmental.

To affirm the value of justice, we need first to confirm the value of *Taqwa* in mind and soul; and to generalise this value so as to make it the core of our management philosophy, we need the unity of the following four wills:

*   the will for political justice
*   the will for economic justice
*   the will for social justice, together with
*   the will for managerial justice.

Hitherto, the main problem in Islamic and Arab societies in modern times has been that there is no such political will on the one hand, and no justice on the other. Hopefully, in countries like Tunisia and Egypt at least, of not also in Jordan, this is now changing.

Sardar says: 'The Muslim world finds itself in a state of helplessness and uncertainty, marginalised, suppressed, angry and frustrated. The condition of Muslim people – the ummah – its subjugation by the west, poverty and dependence, engendered a mood of despondency' (Sardar, 2006).

Of course Sardar was writing in 2006, before the current Awakening. By and large, though, while all Arab and Muslim states have won their independence from colonialism, I do not believe that they are truly independent. There has still been foreign interference in those countries and the justice that was absent then, in colonial if not also pre-colonial times, is still elusive now, in post-colonial times. Other fundamental rights and values are still constrained. Freedom of thought and expression have still been censored and forbidden, which is why Al Jazeera, for example, is a breath of fresh air. On the other hand, while all religions, faiths and ideologies call for justice and freedom, the reality, on the ground, all too often attests to the contrary. Countries and regimes of different faiths and ideologies suppress freedoms and commit injustices, whether inside or outside their countries.

This state of affairs affects the application of justice, as well as freedom and equality, at all levels of the state, including families, communities and organisations, which makes the battle to implement justice and freedom all the more challenging. It is interesting, moreover, that I.Theory has ultimately been evolved by a consulting company, rather than by a university or business school, in the Arab world.

I.Theory in Practice

Some organisations in Jordan besides RSCN and Al-Quds Paints Co. have started to implement I.Theory. These include Future Applied Computer Technology Co., Irbid Electricity Co., Sanabel Landscaping Company, and Tibah Consultants. In general, they chose I.Theory as a background to implementing HR systems, whereby each one built its system in accordance with its particular situation and requirements.

The managers I am working with all have the will to introduce the Islamic concepts within their organisations in order to achieve quality and transformation by using systems based on justice. Muslim people's reaction to Western attacks on Islam, founded or unfounded, have helped us to build new systems originating in our culture.

Implications for My Future Role

The implementation of I.Theory through my consulting practice has led me to focus on values within organisations and to explore how we can move from the global–local (think globally, act locally) to the local–global (evolving local identity towards global integrity) management philosophy through the HR systems I have developed based on I.Theory and Islamic philosophy.

As a management consultant, I can then say the following:

- Relationships between people all too often lead to conflict.
- To minimise this conflict, we need *Taqwa* inside ourselves.
- If we do not enhance the value of *Taqwa* inside ourselves, or the equivalent thereof, we are likely to put ourselves into conflict with others.
- The results of these conflicts lead to loss and damage, socially and economically.

My focus, then, is on justice as a core value in building any relationship, most specifically in a management context, while maintaining balance and equilibrium in the global system in order to attain enhanced civilization–well-being. I feel therefore that I have a very important role to play in working towards organisational transformation. It means working beyond TQM in a way that takes into consideration our culture and beliefs, based on values-managed organisation and justice as an ultimate core value.

How do I sustain the implementation of I.Theory through my work with my clients? In any organisational development consulting assignment, I start with the code of ethics and its implementation, in order to create a foundation within the organisation and propose a core value that the organisation has to follow, through the following three processes:

- An educational process: with the main focus being the total value generated and the core value contained within it, and how to enhance the two together.

- A learning process: to develop employees' knowledge of value and values in the organisation, to enhance the socio-technical integration of their thinking and to understand the organisational ecology, both internal and external.
- A training process: to develop employees' co-operative skills and attitudes.

In summary, I can say that the future for the implementation of I.Theory is a promising one because the concepts and applications related to it are being recommended widely, at least in Jordan. But as I said at the beginning of this chapter, there needs to be a will for justice: a managerial justice will, incorporating an economic justice will, a political justice will and a social justice will. If there are no will and no justice at the higher political levels of our societies, the other three forms of will (managerial, economic and social) will break down and society will live without a local identity and remain underdeveloped.

I.Theory Implementation in Arab and Islamic Societies

Finally, and recently, I have started a series of educational and development programmes for Iraqi and Yemeni nationals on HR systems based on I.Theory. The Iraqis were trained in HR development and the Yemenis in public reform. The two groups sought to build HR systems that conformed to their culture and norms. In all my consulting work and educational projects outside Jordan I present I.Theory and the systems to be built on the basis of Islamic concepts in management. Hopefully, this will be a first step towards the scaling up and renewal of Islamic theories in management.

Bibliography

Abrahamson, Eric. 'Management Fashion', *Academy of Management Review*, Boulder, CO: Leeds School of Business, University of Colorado 1996.

Abu Sheikha, Nader. *Consulting Management*, Amman: Middle East Press Co., 1986.

Aljazar, Amer. *The Group of Fatwa Ibn Taymiyah*, Al-Jihad section, Egypt: Dar Alwafa Press, 1998.

Assaf, Abdelmutti. *I.Theory, the Road to Excellence, Management by Values*, Amman: Wael Press, 2005 (Arabic).

Al-Baqmi, Tami. *Hisba Practices*, Riyad: KSA, 1995.

Block, Peter. *Flow Less Consulting: A Guide to Getting Your Expertise Used*, Austin, TX: Learning Concepts, 1981.

Bukhari, Mohammad. *Saheeh Bukhari*, Damascus: Dar Ibn Katheer, 1993.

Chary, S.N. *Production and Operations Managements*, 3rd edition, New Delhi: Tata McGraw-Hill, 2007.

Al-Daher, Khalid and Tabara, Hasan Mustafa. *Hesba System, Study in Managerial Economics for Islamic Society*, 1st edition, Amman: Dar Almassira Publishers, 1997 (Arabic).

Deming, Edward W. *Out of the Crisis*, Cambridge, MA: MIT Centre for Advanced Educational Services, 1986.

Duncan, W.J. *Management Ideas and Actions*, New York: Oxford University Press, 1999.

'Economy of Jordan', http://encyclopediathefreedictionary.com.

Evans, James and Lindsay, William. *The Management and Control of Quality*, 5th edition, Ohio: South-Western, 2001.

Fayol, H. *Organisational Theory*, Business library, University of Western Ontario, 1981.

Al-Ghazali, Immam Aby Hamid. *Ihya' Ulom Al-deen*, Cairo: 450 AH (CE 1046) (Arabic).

Goetsch, David L. and Davis, Stanley B. *Implementing Total Quality*, Upper Saddle River, NJ: Prentice Hall, 1995.

Goetsch, David L. and Davis, Stanley B. *Quality Management*, 5th edition, Upper Saddle River, NJ: Prentice-Hall, 2002.

Greiner, Larry and Metzger, Robert. *Consulting to Management*, Englewood Cliffs, NJ: Prentice-Hall, 1983.

Hammadi, Hussein. *The Secrets of Japanese Management*, Cairo: Dar Nobar Press, 1988.

Al-Hassaniya, Saleem. *Management Information System (MIS)*, Amman: Al-Warraq Corporation Press, 1997.

Heron, John. *Co-operative Inquiry/Research into the Human Condition*, London: Sage Publications, 1996.

Heron, John. *Feeling and Personhood – Psychology in Another Key*, London: Sage, 1992.

http://1uptraver.com/international/middleeast/Jordan/economy

http://en.wikipedia.org

http://www.danadeclaration.org/text%20website/declarationenglish.html

Inayaatullah, Sohail and Boxwell, Gail. *Sardar, Ziauddin, Islam, Postmodernism and other Futures: A Ziauddin Reader*, London: Pluto Press, 2003.

Ishikawa, K. *What is Total Quality Control?*, trans. D.J. Lu, Englewood Cliffs, NJ: Prentice-Hall, 1985.

Al-Jabri, Mohammed Abed. *Arab Islamic Philosophy: A Contemporary Critique*, Austin, TX: University of Texas Press, 1999.

Juran, J.M. *Juran on Leadership for Quality*, New York: Free Press, 1989.

Khaled, Yehya. 'Transformation Management, 2nd Project', University of Buckingham, UK, 2005 (not published).

Khaled, Yehya. 'Transformation Management, 3rd Project', University of Buckingham, UK, 2006 (not published).

Kuber, Milan (ed.). *Management Consulting, a Guide to the Profession*, 3rd edition, Geneva: International Labour Office, 1996.

Lessem, R. 'The Integral Research', 2004 (unpublished).

Lessem, R. and Schieffer, A. *Transformation Management: Toward the Integral Enterprise*, Farnham: Gower, 2009.

Lessem, R. and Palsule, S. *Re-sourcing Business*, London: Global Integrity Publishing, 2005.

Ministry of Planning, Jordan, www.mop.gov.jo

Nasr, Seyyed Hussein. *The Heart of Islam: Enduring Values for Humanity*, Harper Collins: 2004.

The Holy Qur'an.

Rampersad, Hubert. *Total Performance Scorecard*, Amsterdam: Butterworth, 2003.

Rampersad, Hubert. *Managing Total Quality*, New Delhi: Tata McGraw, 2005

Al-Rasheed, Adel. 'Features of Traditional Arab Management and Organisation in the Jordanian Business Environment', *Journal of Transnational Management Development* (2001) Vol.6, No.1/2, pp. 27–53.

Roys, D., Thyer, B., Padgett, D. and Logan, T. *Total Quality Management Programme Evaluation: An Introduction*, Belmont, CA: Thompson, 2006.

RSCN. *Annual Report*, Amman: RSCN, 2005 (not published).

RSCN. Human Resources Department (not published).

RSCN. Induction File (not published).

RSCN. Reports, 2004 and 2005 (not published).

RSCN. Workshop minutes of meeting, HR Department (not published).

Saheeh Muslim (the Tradition of Prophet Mohammad, Peace be upon him)

Sardar, Ziauddin. *The Future of Muslim Civilisation*, London: Mansell, 1987.

Sardar, Ziauddin. *Islam, Postmodernism and Other Futures*, London: Pluto Press, 2003.

Sardar, Ziauddin. *How Do You Know: Reading Ziauddin Sardar on Islam and Cultural Relations*, London: Pluto Press, 2006.

Seddon, John. *The Case against ISO 9000*, Stevenage, UK: Oak Tree Press, 1997.

Al-Sharabi, Hisham. *Neopatriarchy: A Theory of Distorted Change in Arab Society*, New York: Oxford University Press, 1992.

Al-Sheikh, Badawi. *Total Quality in Islam*, Cairo: Dar Alfiker Alarab, 2000.

Al-Shizari, Abdelrahman Bin Badi, *Nehyat Al-Rutbah fi Talab Al-Hesba. Ultimate Rank in Seeking Quality*, Beirut, 1981. (The author lived in the 14th century CE.)

Society of Automotive Engineers *Quality – Historical Perspective*, Warrendale, PA: SAE, 1981.

Steel, Fritz. *Consulting For Organisational Change*, Amherst, MA: University of Massachusetts Press, 1975.

Takezawa, Shinichi and Whitehill, Arthur M. *Work Ways: Japan and America*, Tokyo: Japanese Institute of Labour, 1984.

Al-Tamimi, Izziddeen Al-Khateeb. *Islam and Contemporary Issues*, Amman: Ministry of Culture, 2003.

Taylor, E. *Primitive Culture*, London: John Murray, 1871

Taylor, F. *The Principles of Scientific Management*, New York and London: Harper Brothers, 1911.

Thurow, Lester. *The Management Challenges: Japanese View*, Cambridge, MA: MIT Press, 1990.

Uselac, Stephen. *Zen Leadership: The Human Side of Total Quality Team Management*, Loundon Vill, OH: Monican, 1993.

Walton, Mary. *The Deming Management Method*, New York: Berkeley Publishing Group, 1986.

Watson, Thomas. *A Business and its Beliefs, the Ideas that Helped Build IBM*, Columbus, OH: McGraw-Hill, 2003

Wilber, K. *Ecology and Spirituality*, Boston, MA: Shambala, 1983.

Yin, Robert. *Case Study Research, Designs and Methods*, London: Sage, 2003.

Bibliography

Appendix 1: Checklist Questionnaire

Quality and Organisational Transformation: Islamic Perspective
Case Study – Royal Society for the Conservation Nature (RSCN)
Co-operative Inquiry Methodology – by John Heron
Checklist for the interviewees at RSCN

A. Experiential

What is your present work at RSCN? Please explain.

How is your work developing?

How do you see your level of involvement and methods?

What is the management style that you implement in your work? Why?

What do you know about international management approaches such as the Western and Japanese approaches?

What are your own management values? What are your Islamic beliefs, or otherwise, regarding work ethics?

Do you believe in transformation management, as a methodology, and in its content? How, what and why?

During your experience of working at RSCN, what has your learning process been?

What feedback can you provide on your experience of working at RSCN?

What do you know about Total Quality Management, and how, if at all, does it connect with Islamic values?

B. Presentational

What opportunities are there to incorporate your vision and ideas at work?

Can you tell me your theoretical scenario for RSCN's transformation?

Which set of values, Islamic or otherwise, would you implement in your scenario?

Would you envision any relationship with the community? If so, would the nature of such a relationship be?

In your scenario, are you part of the RSCN House of Wisdom? In what way?

How do you see the alignment between quality, Islam and transformation?

Do you believe that you have your own management theory for developing a path from global–local to local–global, specifically in relation to quality?

How do you envisage that you might work with other elements of local and global society to further your dreams and aspirations?

C. Propositional

What is your feedback on the transformation process currently being implemented at RSCN, , and your evaluation and assessment of the changes so far?

How do you see RSCN's future?

Do you believe in an Islamic Management Theory (I.Theory)? Can this theory work if put to the test? If so, in what management areas?

What, specifically, is your response to the I.Theory? What are your suggestions for its improvement and development?

How does the concept of quality apply to RSCN? How does it draw from nature and culture in general, and Islamic culture in particular?

What is the alignment, or otherwise, between RSCN's transformational approach and that of the Jordanian government?

How do quality and transformation, from a civic and environmental perspective, compare and contrast with the same in the private and public sectors?

D. Practical

How will you integrate/incorporate your practice with your experiential knowledge?

To what extent do people believe in the practical stage of the transformation process?

Do the staff become motivated as individuals, or as working teams targeting mutual goals? Or are they motivated on the basis of higher religious or spiritual belief that idealise work values?

Are all the staff isolated from, or are they aligned and engaged with society? Or does that depend on their level of management and other factors? Please explain.

Do the staff have the pyramid of knowledge on the ground? If so, does this impact on their level of involvement and help to integrate them in society? To what degree does it give them a human point of view and purpose?

Do you have a mutual agreement between management and staff on conducting all tasks and duties in order to reach specified targets? Do the staff incorporate personal beliefs into their work methods?

Is there real consensus to achieving objectives reflecting an Islamic way of life?

Appendix 2:
Values Indicators According to RSCN Appraisal System

Values Indicators	Self-evaluation					Manager's evaluation				
	Excellent	V. good	Good	Acceptable	Below expectations	Excellent	V. good	Good	Acceptable	Below expectations
1. Strategic achievements										
2. Size of achievements										
3. Commitment to and support of the team decision										
4. Respect and support for other team members										
Third: Continuous Development										
5. Compatibility between skills and duties										
6. Self-development										
7. Benefiting from RSCN training programmes										
8. Contributing to development of other staff										
9. Communication skills										
Fourth: Work Ethics										
10. Honesty and accountability										
11. Environmental ethics										
12. Commitment to RSCN's mission										
13. Compliance with RSCN's procedures										
14. Avoiding conflict of interest										
15. Effective time management										
Fifth: Leadership Skills										
16. Delegation of responsibilities										
17. Team building										
18. Professionalism and fairness between team members										
19. Guiding and motivation of team members										
Total										

Index

If you have found this book useful you may be interested in other titles from Gower

**Transformation Management:
Towards the Integral Enterprise**
Ronnie Lessem and Alexander Schieffer
Hardback: 978-0-566-08896-4
e-book: 978-1-4094-0342-5

**Finance at the Threshold:
Rethinking the Real and Financial Economies**
Christopher Houghton Budd
Hardback: 978-0-566-09211-4
e-book: 978-0-566-09212-1

**Finance and Society in 21st Century China:
Chinese Culture versus Western Markets**
Junie T. Tong
Hardback: 978-1-4094-0129-2
e-book: 978-1-4094-0130-8

GOWER